My Mother's Wedding Dress

The Life and Afterlife of Clothes

Justine Picardie

BLOOMSBURY

Published by Bloomsbury Publishing, New York and London
Distributed to the trade by Holtzbrinck Publishers

All papers used by Bloomsbury Publishing are natural,
recyclable products made from wood grown in well-managed
forests. The manufacturing processes conform to the
environmental regulations of the country of origin.

Library of Congress Cataloging-in-Publication Data

Picardie, Justine.
My mother's wedding dress : the life and afterlife of clothes / Justine
Picardie.—1st U.S. ed.
p. cm.

ISBN-13: 978-1-59691-149-9 (hardcover)
ISBN-10: 1-59691-149-2 (hardcover)

1. Wedding costumes. 2. Clothing and dress. 3. Fashion. 4. Fashion designers.
I. Title.

GT1752.P53 2006
392.5'4—dc22
2005033215

First U.S. Edition 2006

1 3 5 7 9 10 8 6 4 2

Typeset by Hewer Text UK Ltd
Printed in the United States of America by Quebecor World Fairfield

For my mother

"A consultation last year took me to an intelligent and unembarrassed-looking girl. Her style of dressing is disconcerting; where women's clothes are normally attended to down to the last pleat, one of her stockings is hanging down and two buttons of her blouse are open."

Sigmund Freud, *The Interpretation of Dreams*

"She immediately stepped into the wardrobe and got in among the coats and rubbed her face against them, leaving the door open, of course, because she knew that it is very foolish to shut oneself into any wardrobe."

C. S. Lewis, *The Lion, the Witch and the Wardrobe*

"Have you ever been so lonely that you felt eternally guilty—as if you'd left off part of your clothes—I love you so, and being without you is like having gone off and left the gas-heater burning, or locked the baby in the clothes-bin."

letter from Zelda Fitzgerald to her husband, Scott Fitzgerald

CONTENTS

1

My Mother's Wedding Dress

"Married in black, you will wish yourself back."

MY MOTHER WAS married in a black wedding dress, a French cocktail dress from an expensive boutique in Hampstead, close to where she lived at the time. It was October 1960, the beginning of many things: the winter, the decade, the marriage, and me. I was born eight months later, in June 1961, feet first and too small (little enough to fit into a bottom drawer, until a cot could be found; five pounds of jaundiced fretfulness; not the neatly stitched white-linen contents of the bottom drawer that my mother's mother would have planned). When I was eighteen and started to wear the dress—a narrow, corseted sheath, just above knee-length, hidden bones within its bodice and waist—I thought about my mother, and how slender she had been on her wedding day, no more than a girl herself, even though she was meant to be all grown up.

What became of the black dress? It has gone and disappeared, lost like my parents' marriage, yet it lives on in my memory, and in photographs of my mother's wedding day, and of me, when I wore it to my university graduation ceremony, a few weeks before my twenty-first birthday. Just as I cannot yet explain how or why or when I allowed such a precious bequest to slip through my fingers, neither can my mother tell me her precise reasons for buying the dress (and sometimes, when I wake up in the night and think about this, about what I don't know, and what I want to know, it feels as if something has unraveled within and without me). But what my mother can recall for me is this: she spent more, far more, on her wedding dress than anything else in her wardrobe; sixty pounds, which was a great deal of money in those days, especially for an impoverished twenty-one-year-old, newly arrived in London from South Africa.

"I bought it in a hurry," she says.

"Why black?" I ask her.

"Why not?" she says.

Although the wedding dress was lined with a soft dark silk—worn and torn by the time I inherited it, wrinkling like an older woman's skin—its skirt was made of a scratchy woolen mohair beneath a satin bodice. I sometimes wonder if my mother hoped it would keep her warm, in the unfamiliar coldness of London, even though the dress was sleeveless and really rather short. "I thought it would be useful," she says. To which I might reply, "How useful is a French cocktail dress to a pregnant girl living in a rented one-bedroom flat in Hampstead?"

But that would be missing the point entirely. The dress, perhaps, was her way of declaring that she was a chic European now; that she had left behind the safe conformity of her colonial upbringing (a place more English than England, with its good manners and carefully observed social etiquette). Here was my mother—a pale-faced convent girl, with a family tree that was carefully traced back to a beatified Catholic martyr; the great-granddaughter of a colonel of the 11th Hussars—marrying a Jew. I was always taught never to say that word; to say "Jewish" instead, to avoid the inflections of anti-Semitism; but isn't this how the story of my parents' wedding would have been told at the time, back home in South Africa? Hilary Garnett married Michael Picardie, a Jew, in London, in black.

Actually, I can't be certain how that story was told. South Africa was such a long way away—and when we did go there to visit my mother's parents, Pat and Fred, they were far too polite to comment on their daughter's marriage. They were not wealthy, despite the titles and prosperity of previous generations on both sides of their family ("I'm a Balfour," my grandmother used to say, with some pride, "and your grandfather is a Garnett," not that those names meant anything to me). Pat and Fred are dead now, leaving me a set of Georgian silver cutlery and a clutch of unanswered questions; as discreetly silent in death as in life; though I have borrowed from my mother a map to their lost world, a copy of the Garnett family tree. My mother is not certain who wrote it ("One of the unmarried aunts, I think," she says, "a grand one in South Kensington"), but I have pored over the author's spidery Edwardian handwriting in order to decipher a small piece of the fabric of my past. It seems that my grandfather Fred was the son of a second son: his father had come to South Africa, lured there by the goldmines, but there was no fortune to be found, just blackwater fever, which killed my great-grandfather at the age of forty, leaving behind him a widow, May, and two children, Lillian and Fred. Someone had to support the family (and May, said to be a stubborn sort, didn't want charity from the rich relatives back home in England), so my grandfather left school at fifteen and trained to be an engineer. He was a man who liked mending things, who could fix anything: even a broken heart, it seemed to me whenever my sister and I went to stay with my grandparents; not that my mother would have necessarily agreed.

Pat and Fred loved each other with a calm consistency quite unlike my own parents' marriage, and their lives were ruled by routine: up with the sun, the BBC World Service news just after breakfast, *The Times* crossword, tea and shortbread at 11 a.m. and half-past three; a brandy sundowner at six. The only disagreement of theirs I ever witnessed was over the last slice of avocado in a green salad: they both loved avocado, and wanted the other to enjoy the remaining piece. "You have it," said Fred to Pat; "No *you* have it," she replied, and so it went on, back and forth, until the excessive courtesy seemed suddenly to infuriate them, and my grandmother tried to throw the avocado onto my grandfather's plate, but missed, so that it fell onto the pristine white table cloth, green and smearing. What did Pat say then? Did she purse her lips, or laugh, shame-faced? Did the stain come out in the wash? Probably, scrubbed clean by my house-proud grandmother, though it remains on the linen forever for me, fixed there in memory, indelible, when so much else has faded away.

Despite the constancy in other parts of their life, Pat and Fred did not stay put in their houses. When I was a child, they moved from Cape Town to Johannesburg, to and fro, several times, like stately migrating birds (following similar patterns, perhaps, to their parents and grandparents, Victorian and Edwardian colonials, who crossed oceans and continents, Australia, India, Africa, with no visible sign of complaint). But their wardrobes always seemed to stay the same: my grandfather's dark suits, neatly pressed, and his ironed white cotton shirts, kept in their place, to one side of my grandmother's equally respectable starched separates and modest neutral frocks. Of my grandmother's wedding dress there was no sign, not even a picture on the mahogany sideboard. She hated being photographed, complained always of her ugliness in front of a camera, and destroyed dozens of pictures as a result, but my mother managed to rescue one page from an album, which shows Pat in what looks like a long lace dress and a wide-brimmed hat. ("A beautiful coffee-colored lace dress," my mother says, "I used to admire it so much as a little girl, and then one day it disappeared. Whatever can have become of it?")

Beneath the photograph, my grandmother has written, "THE DAY 25–10–1930." "The" is underlined with four neat lines, each one shorter than the other, so that it descends into an arrowhead. I know this is my grandmother's handwriting—I recognize it instantly, from all the airmail letters she sent us from South Africa, thin blue paper, covered with thin blue lines. When I look at the arrow now, it seems to lead somewhere else, to another day, an undated day, the first day that I remember, from that almost unimaginable time before my sister was born. My mother was pregnant, so it must have been 1964, maybe the end of '63, and I was just about two, and we had flown, without my father, to stay with her parents in South Africa. I remember the airplane—or more specifically, the glamour of its air hostess, who wore a jaunty hat and polished high heels, and had a little curtained annex of her own, with a mirror where she let me try on her lipstick—and I remember my grandparents' wardrobe. It was big, large enough for me to climb into it, and I stayed there, my cheeks against their lavender-scented clothes, until they called me outside to see a parade that was going past the window. (Recently, when I ask my mother if I am imagining things, she laughs, and says it's true, I did sit in the wardrobe, and sometimes my grandmother played with me in there, while I pretended to be an air hostess. "And there was a parade, of sorts. It was Christmas, and the Salvation Army band came and did a concert outside on the street." My mother is silent for a moment, and then says, "I wish I could remember their address . . .")

As for my father's parents: I never really knew them at all. Like Pat and Fred, they were émigrés, but from a very different place. They had escaped from Lithuania and Russia, ending up on ships to Cape Town, though they might as easily have gone to Liverpool or London or New York instead. My father's mother, whose name was Minnie, died when I was still very young, and his father, Granddad Louis, was in disgrace, having remarried a blonde shiksa called Marilyn, and frittered away the family's hard-earned savings and investments. I wish I had known Louis better—he was a poet and schoolteacher who abandoned Judaism and turned to spiritualism and séances instead, much to his family's annoyance—but I do have a photograph of him and Minnie that I treasure; a sepia picture of them on their wedding day. Her face is turned towards the camera, looking straight out at me, and she is wearing an elaborate white gown: long-sleeved and lacy, with a train gathered over one arm, and a big bouquet of creamy roses. She has two strings of pearls around her neck, and more pearls wound around her white headdress. She is beautiful, like a still of a silent movie star. Louis is in a dark suit and a high-collared stiff white shirt, gazing at his wife, apparently rapt at her beauty. My youngest son, who has seen this photograph on the mantelpiece of my study, says that Louis looks sinister, a bit like Dracula, ready to bite his bride's neck.

I don't think so; I think he was just counting his blessings that day.

I have searched for the same look on my father's face in the pictures of my parents' wedding day: he is darkly handsome, like Louis, beside his sweet-faced smiling bride. They hardly knew each other—had met only twelve weeks before, in London; drawn together, perhaps, by what they had left behind in South Africa, even though their paths had never crossed in their homeland. Their parents were not at the wedding, and neither was my mother's twin brother—it was a quiet ceremony, in Hampstead registry office, witnessed by my mother's older brother, Richard, and their auntie Lil (Fred's sister Lillian, who lived in London, having escaped South Africa, leaving a husband behind). Lil is wearing her pearls, and Richard and my father are in buttoned-up dark suits; my father's from a Savile Row tailor, made for him when he first came to England on a student scholarship to Oxford. Richard's tie is neatly knotted, as is the collar of his shirt, but my father is more rumpled: his striped tie does not sit quite as it should beneath his collar, as if he had wrestled with it the morning of his wedding day. The pictures are black and white, so I cannot see the color of his tie, or my mother's cloud of red hair, which nevertheless looks like a Renaissance angel's halo in the flash of the camera. To one side, above my father's cropped black curls, there is a blurring of white light (which my grandfather Louis would doubtless have seen as spiritual; evidence of the Other Side, come through to witness the ceremony). This light is there in all four of the photographs that I have of the wedding: pictures I have examined over and over again, like separate pieces of a jigsaw, that might eventually fit together and make more sense. In the first picture, my parents are smiling at one another, standing in front of the door to what I guess is the registry office; in the second, the door is open, and they are smiling at the camera, and I can see there is a rose pinned to my mother's dress, and rather disconcertingly, a stranger's face, hovering between their shoulders, like a materialized ghost in a Victorian photograph. In what I think of as the third picture (not that there is an order to them, apart from my own), they are sitting inside the registrar's office; Richard next to my mother, and my father on the other end of the sofa. Lil is behind them, standing, and my mother is leaning towards my father, though my father has both his hands on his suited knees, looking rather disapproving, looking like the angry young man he was in those days, a political radical, a member of the ANC. In the final photograph, my parents are alone again, close up, leaving the registry office. They seem to be holding hands, but it's hard to tell—their fingers don't seem to be doing the right thing—and my mother is turned to my father, with a nervous not-smile, and my father is gazing at something else, away from the camera, something unseen in the middle distance. The photographs are stuck very tightly to the black paper pages of the album in which they are kept (glued there by my maternal grandparents, I think, who would have been sent them in South Africa; and then posted all the way back to London to my mother, months or even years later, probably). But just now, I lifted a corner of one of them, the last picture, and there, in tiny silver hand-writing, the neatest capital letters, someone has written: "JUST YOU TRY!"

I never saw my mother wearing her black wedding dress again; and it never did come in useful for her, as a party outfit or otherwise, as far as I could see. But she kept it safely, despite all the moves we made—from Hampstead to the English countryside (so cold, that winter, she remembers, stuck in a cottage in the middle of snowbound fields in rural Oxford-shire; no way out for weeks at a time), and then to Liverpool, where my father was studying for a while, and south to Henley-on-Thames (how weird was *that* for a couple of young radicals?), and to London again, to a flat in Marylebone High Street, and afterward to Oxford, where my father got a job as a university lecturer. Oh, and there were more moves—too many for me to remember—but the wedding dress came with her, even when my father did not.

The dress had a little matching jacket with it that buttoned up at the back, so neat and perfectly cut that when it was worn over the dress, you wouldn't necessarily guess that bare flesh was beneath; that something sleeveless was going on. My mother kept the jacket on during her wedding day, at least she did in the photographs; so perhaps it was me who turned the outfit into a party dress; jacketless, wanton, feeling myself to have been set free in a way that she was not. I don't remember my mother actually *giving* me the dress: I think I'd found it for myself one day, looking through her wardrobe. I'd always been interested in her clothes—they seemed to be material clues to her history, and mine; more significant, perhaps, because there were relatively few to examine. She was very frugal, unlike my sister and me when we grew up, and after this one extravagance for her wedding day, bought herself little in the way of party outfits, though she made wonderfully exuberant dresses for us as children, which seemed like the most precious of gifts.

I'm not certain of the precise circumstances in which I first wore her wedding dress—but I remember the way it felt, stepping into it, holding my breath, while someone—my mother or my sister?—zipped it up at the back for me; and fastened hooks and eyes, too (for this was a dress that I could not put on or take off without help). It must have been shortly afterward that I packed the dress into a battered suitcase when I left home, at eighteen, to go to Cambridge—a place where I thought I could reinvent myself, leave my family behind. But my running-away bag contained bits and pieces of my mother: not just the dress, but an old bone-handled bread knife, a brightly colored blanket she had brought with her as a girl from South Africa, and her handwritten recipe for scones. My mother has very precise handwriting, small and carefully formed, and she wrote postcards to me at university, a time of great unhappiness in her life, though her sadness was kept between the lines. Her marriage had been tempestuous, marked by separations and reconciliations and several attempts at fresh starts, but now it was finally at an end. She was forty, and I had gone, taking her wedding dress with me.

At university, I tended only to wear old clothes, other people's clothes: mainly stuff that I bought for very little money, from the stalls in Cambridge market. That might sound dismal, but the clothes were as exuberant as I was. There was a frilly rose-pink sixties dress—layered, like petals, its pastel sweetness sabotaged by the fact that it was almost indecently short, especially when I cycled home in it, drunk and weaving under the wide night sky, my party face covered in the kisses of boys I had left behind. (One night, a policeman stopped me, and said I shouldn't be out so late alone, dressed like that; and I just laughed, and said I was too fast to catch.) I also bought fifties cotton frocks—splashed with flowers, vivid pinks and greens, daisies running riot—and sparkling sequined cardigans that smelled of mothballs and cologne; and a long tulle ball gown, sherbet-lemony skirts cascading from its tightly fitted waist. I wore other women's shoes, too, still bearing the shape of their feet; precipitous heels from twenty years ago, sixties lilac satin stilettos and black patent winkle-pickers and fake crocodile boots. It was all so cheap, but I treasured these things, my trove from jumble sales and charity shops, washed up into my arms.

If the contents of one's wardrobe are in any way the manifestation of one's inner self (which I believe them to be, some of the time, at least), then mine was a rag-tag bundle of other people's identities, assembled into something of my own. All those second-hand clothes are gone now, abandoned or lost or fallen apart; and I mourn none of them, not deeply, except the wedding dress. I feel that in losing it, the past is eluding me; as if I have lost a piece of my heart.

2

The Fairy Without Any Knickers On

"I'm Nobody! Who are you?
Are you—Nobody—Too?
Then there's a pair of us?
Don't tell! they'd advertise—you know!"
Emily Dickinson, poem 288

"Clothes serve to cover the body, and thus gratify the impulse
to modesty. But, at the same time, they may enhance the
beauty of the body, and indeed, as we have seen, this was
probably their most primitive function . . . In fact, the whole
psychology of clothes undergoes at once a great clarification
and a great simplification, if this fundamental ambivalence in
our attitude be fully grasped and continually held in mind."
J. C. Flugel, *The Psychology of Clothes*

THERE HAS TO BE a first dress, like a first kiss; there has to be.
Mine was the one that my mother made for me to wear to my
birthday party: a fairy dress, sewn of translucent net, with
matching wings and a glittery silver wand. I was three, and my
sister was still a baby, and we were living in a place called
Damer Gardens, a modestly modern housing estate in Henley-
on-Thames. There were lots of other children who lived
there—a nursery tribe of us—and our house was in a cul-

de-sac, just off the main circle of houses; safe enough for me to ride my tricycle around the road with my friends; but also a place that seemed to lead to somewhere more dangerous, as well. (Outside the circle, behind a hedge, there was a man—The Man—who hid from us, just as we hid from him, but if he were to see me, or I to see him, then I knew I would be stolen away, or worse. Did I ever glimpse him? I think I did, just once, blurred and wild and half naked, but I can't be sure, it might have been a dream; a nightmare, like the nightmares we all share, of being undressed, of disgrace . . .)

When I think back to that time, try to see it clearly (as if clarity were possible, and the smudges wiped clean), the memory is tinged with a kind of shame and secrecy, even though I am running through it, in sunshine and summer light. My birthday is in midsummer—the day before the shortest night of the year—and warm, so that my party is to be held in the garden. Someone (who? I can't remember who) has told me that I do not need to wear any knickers beneath my fairy dress—that I must take them off, because they will show through the net—and then when all my guests are assembled, before the party games have begun, the boldest of them, a boy, points at me and cries, "You don't have any knickers on!" When he says this, I know that I have done something wrong and been caught out; but I cannot speak, I am hot and humiliated, I hate myself, I feel like an ugly goblin.

The fairy dress is my first lesson in what can be uncovered, and what must be covered up. Well, I'd like to believe it was that simple (a discovery, like the sartorial clues in a Hitchcock film), but it isn't, of course, because I still haven't worked out the threads of the past, have not got everything sewn up. Also, when I remember the fairy dress, it reminds me of the story of the Emperor's new clothes: at least, my tangled childish version of it, in which I imagined the Emperor dressed up in his finery—not naked at all—but underneath his new clothes, there was nothing; truly, nothing, no skin, no flesh, no bones, just emptiness. And from then on, I knew that nobody meant exactly that: *no body*, a condition that might be hidden by clothes.

The fairy dress and the Emperor's new clothes collide in my mind, perhaps, because they coincide with my learning to read and write: once upon a time, at home, all of a sudden the letters turn into words. I make lots of mistakes—where do the circles go; which letters have cul-de-sacs?—but even so, the books provide a safe place, behind their covers, where no one will see me, or shame me, where I can disappear, hidden by others' words. There is another hiding place, too: a wooden Wendy House set on stilts in our back garden; Wendy is a girl in a book and she flies away from home, but she knows her mother will be waiting for her. Her father is in the doghouse, chained up, so he cannot do anything, poor man. (Later, much later, my mother tells me about Wendy growing too big for her little house, and her arms and legs are poking out of it, so she looks like she is wearing a dress that has shrunk in the wash; and I say no, that was Alice in Wonderland, after she has eaten the cake that made her suddenly expand.) Wendy is briefly captured, and so am I, in photographs: cradling my baby sister, my baby; sitting with her on my lap in the garden outside. Inside our house, my parents have two antique chairs—we call them "the thrones"—of a dark ebonized wood inlaid with mother of pearl. One day, my sister and I are photographed sitting on the chairs, separately. Ruth can sit up now by herself. She has dark curls and dark eyes, like my father, and I look more like my mother, but even so, our faces seem to reflect each other, so that we two are one. On the back of my throne, above and behind my head, the pearl makes patterns and pictures: circles of leaves and two white winged horses, facing each other, ready to fly, but they are inside the picture on the chair, and they are always there, they cannot break free.

In the photograph, I am wearing a dress with a dark background, covered in sprigs of white flowers and bright orange blooms, as if I am growing out of the throne, sprouting yet rooted to it. There is a narrow crocheted trimming around the neck and bodice and fluted bell-sleeves. In my hands, I am holding the treasured shell of a sea urchin, which has come all the way from Africa. The dress has come from Africa, too, given to me by one of my father's aunts, a hand-me-down from her daughter; flown here over the desert and the ocean, even though it has no wings. It is short, almost too small for me to wear now, and my legs are crossed; hollow legs, my mum says, as I get taller. The shell is very precious and fragile, hollow inside, like my legs (its previous inhabitant, the sea urchin, dead and gone). I know I must not drop the shell, for it would break into a hundred little pieces, and nobody would be able to glue it together again; not like my flowering dress from Africa, which has been mended and darned.

Why are these clothes so etched upon my imagination, as if history can be pieced together by a patchwork of this stuff? When I try to get things straight in my head—to tell the story properly, as stories should be told—it seems impossible to un-jumble; though maybe memory is not a jumble, but a kind of loom, shuttling through the warp and the weft, weaving together a whole. After the fairy dress, I'd like to think that all my other dresses were armor, keeping me safe inside, but there's always a chink, isn't there? I can see that, clearly, when my mother makes me a crocheted silver skirt: full of tiny holes in the gleaming metallic Lurex knit. I wear it when we leave Henley-on-Thames and move to London, to a flat in Marylebone High Street. I am living high above the High Street, sleeping on the top bunk in the bedroom I share with Ruth. The room is painted purple, like my mother's favorite minidress; the bathroom is sprayed silver, like my skirt.

Ruth and I have a dressing-up box in the bedroom. The fairy dress is in there, but I don't like it now, it's too scratchy, it itches, as if it has left an invisible mark on my skin. It stays at the bottom of the box, in the dark, while I go out, because I have left nursery, I am at Robinsfield Infants' School, and one day a journalist visits the playground, to ask us what we think about heaven. "People have bare skins," I tell him, amongst other things, and I spell it out for him, B-A-R-E, not B-E-A-R, like my teacher taught me, but when he writes his article, it comes out differently. I didn't read it at the time, but I do now, all these years later, because my grandmother cut it out of a magazine, and stuck it into a photograph album, the one I have inherited. It's a tiny cutting from the October 1968 edition of the *Reader's Digest*, which my grandparents subscribed to. The *Reader's Digest* has digested my words from a much earlier edition of the *Daily Mail*. This is what I am supposed to have said, aged five: "In heaven the people are mummies and daddies and children. There are square houses, round houses and tall houses. The ladies have skirts on only because it is so hot. Men wear only shorts. There is a lot of singing about God because He lives there and He is the King." There is no mention of the bare skins, or bearskins, in this misinterpreted Eden.

Meanwhile, back home, in our earthly eyrie, my sister and I wear the princess dresses that our grandmother has sent from South Africa. The dresses say "PRINCESS" on the label, and they are long and many-layered, pink and peach, and they crackle when we pull them over our heads. My mother says this is called "static electricity," but it seems more like magic to me, the buzzing of fairies outside and inside my head. "Why does she send me a nylon nightie every Christmas and every birthday?" says my mother, one corner of her mouth curved in a smile. "What does she think I wear in bed?" My mother does not wear the Princess presents from my grandmother, so Ruth and I dress up in them instead.

I want to be a princess, and I am reading *The Lion, the Witch and the Wardrobe*. One day, I hope, we will be like Susan and Lucy, the sisters in the book: if Ruth and I sit long enough in the right wardrobe, and fall through the other side into Narnia, we will live happily ever after, with the fauns and centaurs and talking animals. (The trouble is, how do I know we have the right wardrobe? Maybe it's the wrong one; not that I have any choice . . .) Lucy finds her way to Narnia, beyond the fur coats and the mothballs in a wardrobe in an otherwise empty room, one of many in the house that she is staying in ("the sort of house that you never seem to come to the end of . . . full of unexpected places"). At first, her sister and brothers think she has imagined this other world, ruled by the White Witch who is beautiful but deadly in her robes of white fur, and then they discover that Narnia is real.

I believe in Aslan, the lion who saves Narnia, who will save us all. When my tooth falls out, he comes padding along Marylebone High Street in the darkness, and he climbs up the stairs into our flat, and when everyone is sleeping, he takes my tooth and leaves me a sixpence behind. Aslan can speak, but he is silent on his visits to London, so quiet that he never wakes us; but I know that he will protect me when I walk to school through the park, like he watches over the children in Narnia.

My dad listens to a song about Lucy in the sky with diamonds, he plays it on the record player, over and over again; but his Lucy is not the right one, she doesn't go to Narnia. The real Lucy, my Lucy (who found her way through the wardrobe, not into the sky), has a little bottle made of diamond, containing within it a cordial of the juice of the fire-flowers that grow in the mountains of the sun. If she or her sister is hurt, a few drops of it will cure them. And she has a dagger.

I would like a dagger or a gun, like Bonnie who is the girl in my other favorite book, *The Wolves of Willoughby Chase* by Joan Aiken. Bonnie doesn't have a sister, but she has a cousin, Sylvia, who comes to live with her in Willoughby Chase, a great house with battlements and turrets, that stands in eminence in the heart of the wold. That's what it's called, the wold, but I read it as the world. Bonnie is the only daughter of Sir Willoughby and Lady Green, who are kind and loving parents, but they must leave her for a long voyage, in search of a cure for her mother's illness. Lady Green is pale and ailing and beautiful, but in her place arrives an evil fourth cousin, Miss Slighcarp, to take charge of Bonnie and Sylvia as their governess and guardian. Sylvia is an orphan, who has been raised by her Aunt Jane in an attic room in Park Lane, and she travels by train to Willoughby Chase with a suitcase of clothes sewn by her aunt out of an old curtain of white Chinese brocade. "I do like to see a little girl dressed all in white," says Aunt Jane, as she weeps over Sylvia's going-away clothes.

Sylvia is rather depressed at the thought of wearing only white, but she would never dream of saying so, for she is a good child (as I am); and anyway, Aunt Jane also makes her a traveling cloak of green velvet, cut from the shawl that they have slept beneath on cold nights in Park Lane. Aunt Jane is left with nothing to warm her but a jet-trimmed mantle, and Sylvia departs in shabby shoes, polished with a mix of soot and candle grease, in a bonnet trimmed with a white plume from the ostrich-feather fan that her aunt had carried at her coming-out ball. (At eight, I never questioned why Aunt Jane had fallen on such hard times, while her relatives lived in splendor; though now it seems as inexplicable as the sudden impoverishment of my grandfather Fred, sent out to work at fifteen to support his mother and sister while his wealthy English cousins played cricket at Eton and went skiing in Gstaad.)

As for Miss Slighcarp: she arrived in Willoughby Chase clad from head to toe in a traveling dress of swathed gray twill, with a stiff collar, dark glasses, and dull green buttoned boots. The day after Bonnie's parents have departed on their travels, Miss Slighcarp appears wearing one of Lady Green's dresses: a draped gown of old gold velvet with ruby buttons. When Bonnie demands that the governess takes off her mother's dress, there is a struggle, and a bottle of ink is knocked over, spilling a long blue trail down the gold velvet. I remember all this, in far more detail than my own parents' fierce arguments, where burning pans are snatched from the cooker and thrown at one another, and clothes are torn, along with everything else; because I have read and reread *The Wolves of Willoughby Chase*, until I know it almost by heart. Clothes, it seems to me, are the signs and signals by which a child might recognize and avoid danger, or defeat the enemies all around. For there are human wolves, as well as the packs that hunt on Willoughby Wold; and sometimes they wear sheepskin, and sometimes they come in fur.

Best-Dressed Heroines

1. Pippi Longstocking: carrot-colored pigtails, blue dress with little red patches sewn on by herself, long stockings (one brown, the other black), giant black shoes, twice as long as her feet; though Pippi is never too big for her boots. (And her creator, Astrid Lindgren, has never been bettered; for once encountered, Pippi Longstocking is always remembered; the nine-year-old who lives alone, with a horse on the porch and a monkey on her shoulder, who waves to her angel-mother in heaven, saying, "Don't worry, I can look after myself!")

2. Kate, in Rosamond Lehmann's *Invitation to the Waltz*, at a coming-out ball in 1920: "The airy apple-green frock which Kate made for herself flared out below her hips and clung lightly to waist and breast. A little floating cape was attached just over each flat delicately-moulded shoulder-blade by a band of minute flowers, buds, leaves of all colours." Most impressively, Kate "just took it straight from *Vogue*."

3. Holly Golightly in Truman Capote's *Breakfast at Tiffany's*: not simply because of her perfect little black dress, black sandals and pearls, but because of how she wears them, with "a soap and lemon cleanness" and "the ragbag colors of her boy's hair," tawny streaked and blonde.

4. Rebecca, as imagined by the second Mrs. de Winter; Daphne du Maurier's day-dreamed glamorous ghost, in the silver dress glimpsed in a dead woman's living wardrobe.

5. Linda in *The Pursuit of Love*; though not only as dressed by Paris couturiers. Before then—before her affair with the fabulous Fabrice—she is a 1930s debutante with a talent for looking original: "Linda had one particularly ravishing ball-gown made of masses of pale grey tulle down to her feet. Most of the dresses were still short that summer, and Linda made a sensation whenever she appeared in her yards of tulle, very much disapproved of by Uncle Matthew, on the grounds that he had known three women burnt to death in tulle ball-dresses." (Could Nancy Mitford have remembered that the Reverend Patrick Brontë, father of his more famous Brontë daughters, was similarly fearful of inflammable gowns?)

6. Cassandra, narrator of my favorite novel, *I Capture the Castle* by Dodie Smith, and her sister, Rose, who dye all their clothes green at the beginning of the novel, to make up for the fact that they are penniless; Rose wears their stepmother's hand-me-down silk tea gown, "which looked wonderful—it had been a faded blue, but had dyed a queer sea-green."

7. Flora Poste and Elfine Starkadder in Stella Gibbons's *Cold Comfort Farm*. Flora—a wonderfully dressed, wonderfully wise and witty heroine—takes her younger cousin, Elfine, in hand: "A large girl like you *must* wear clothes that *fit*; and Elfine, *whatever* you do, always wear court shoes. Remember—c-o-u-r-t. You are so handsome that you can wear the most conventional clothes and look very well in them; but do, for heaven's sake, avoid orange linen jumpers and hand-wrought jewelry. Oh, and shawls in the evening." Flora subsequently changes Elfine's life by taking her to London, to be fitted for a ball gown ("She bathed

delightedly in white satin, like a swan in foam"). At the party that follows, "Flora's own dress was in harmonious tones of pale and dark green. She wore no jewels, and her long coat was of viridian velvet . . . Flora knew that she did not look so beautiful as Elfine, but, then, she did not want to. She knew that she looked distinguished, elegant, and interesting. She asked for nothing more."

8. The Girls of Slender Means, in Muriel Spark's novel of the same name, who share among themselves a single Schiaparelli taffeta evening dress: a "marvelous dress, which caused a stir wherever it went . . . It was colored dark blue, orange and white in a floral pattern as from the Pacific Islands."

9. Esther, the narrator of Sylvia Plath's autobiographical novel *The Bell Jar*, skinny as a boy and naked beneath her black shantung sheath, in a hot New York summer working for a fashion magazine. (Inspiration for Edie Sedgwick, and others in a later sixties line-up of the Beautiful and Damned?)

10. Miss Havisham in *Great Expectations*. Yes, I know she looks appalling in her ancient wedding dress and tattered bridal veil, but she is also the most memorably dressed woman in any of Dickens' novels (and possibly rather influential: emulated in all those successive waves of vintage chic, and on the catwalk, too, in Commes des Garçons' autumn/winter 2005 show); and no one could ever forget her terrible ending, ablaze with a crown of fire soaring above her head.

11. Mrs. Ada Harris, the heroine of Paul Gallico's *Mrs. 'arris Goes to Paris*; though perhaps she should be in a category all of her own. A widowed London cleaning lady of sixty

or so, she scrimps and saves enough money to travel to Paris to buy a Dior dress, of "wonderous frothy foam of seashell pink, sea-cream and pearl white." It cannot transform her into a beautiful young girl—"the creation worked no miracles, except in her soul"; but its magic survives, despite damage and misadventure, so that by the end of the story, "Mrs. Harris hugged the dress to her thin bosom, hugged it hard as though it were alive and human . . ."

3

The Orange Apple Dress

THE APPLE DRESS isn't green, nor any kind of apple-y color, it's flaming orange, even brighter than my mother's burnished copper-red hair. She has taken me to the Apple shop, on Baker Street, around the corner from our flat. The Apple shop is owned by the Beatles, she says, you know, *the Beatles*; and I do know, I nearly saw them one day, driving past us in a white Rolls-Royce, sprayed with painted rainbows. My mum said, "Look, that's the Beatles." I looked, but they were gone so fast, I couldn't see them, just their big car, swooping away, while my mouth fell open, in a silent "oh." But I can see them on the cover of my parents' records. I like *Sergeant Pepper's Lonely Hearts Club Band*; I sing along to the songs, I know all the words, I know about the spaces to leave between the lines ("Look for the girl with the sun in her eyes, and she's gone . . ." boom, boom, boom); and I like their Sergeant Pepper clothes, the bright colors and gold-brocaded uniforms. My mum explains it to me: Ringo is wearing the pink suit, John is in the yellow one, that's Paul in blue, and George in the orangey-red, with a matching hat on his head. My dress is more orange than George's suit, but it's hard to see the color properly in the Apple shop, which is dark inside, like a cave, smoky and bat-dark, full of people who seem to be half-asleep, lolling on the ground, like the slumped blurred shapes of grown-ups who fill our flat, occasionally, the morning after my parents' parties.

Outside, the dress is more astonishing, with tiny mirrors sewn down the front, glittering in the light, like tiny eyes, I think to myself, like Lucy in the sky with diamonds. The mirrors are too small for me to see myself in, but I imagine the outside world reflected in my dress, broken up into pieces, lots of little bits of beyond. It is July 1969, the summer holidays have nearly started, and I am wearing my orange dress because it is a special day—a dressing-up day—when my mum has taken Ruth and me to see the Rolling Stones play a concert in Hyde Park. I can't remember if my dad is there; I can't remember much, to be honest, apart from the mirrors on the orange Apple dress, and Mick Jagger's smock. He is a man wearing a white dress—a tiny little man, more like a dancing doll or a marionette, a long way away on the stage—but when we get closer, pushing through the crowd, past more people than I have ever imagined, we see some white butterflies around him, hundreds of butterflies, fluttering to the ground, like falling angels. It is very sad, my mum says, because someone has died; another man who left the Rolling Stones is dead, Brian Jones is dead, and it looks to me like the butterflies are dying, as well. (You must never touch their wings, I tell my sister. If you touch a butterfly's wings, it won't be able to fly again, and that will be the end of it.)

At home, my dad is also very sad. He feels like death, he says. One day he is looking at his books on the shelves in the living room; but the shelves aren't straight, he says, and he starts crying. "I'm going under," he says, "I'm going down."

There are tears rolling down his cheeks, and there is nothing I can do to make them stop, there is nothing, he says; and my mirrored dress is very thin, I feel cold inside, shivery and unarmed, and he is shivering, too.

Not long afterward, my mum's best friend comes to live with us in the flat. Sometimes she cries, as well, because she and her husband have split up (a phrase which sounds like splintered wood to me; like broken bookshelves). But selfishly, I'm happy that she is here, with her two children: a small boy who is the same age as my sister, and a baby girl, all of us squashed together in our little flat, like a lifeboat leaving the scene of a sinking ship; enough of us to keep more accidents from happening, enough to keep us afloat.

We go for picnics in Regent's Park, beside the lake where the ducks swim, their feathers all glossy and shining, skirting and squawking past queenly black swans. I lie on the grass and look up through the trees, through the patterned leaves, the sunlight turning green, like being underwater. My mum and her friend murmur in soft voices, too muffled for me to hear the words, and the little ones climb over me, tumbling and rolling across the grass. We walk to and from the park, over Marylebone Road, crossing at the same place every time, beneath the circle of gold angels that are gathered around the St. Marylebone church tower. I always remember to look up at them, and they are always there, unmoved yet poised for flight, surveying the city from their perches in the sky.

At home, there is the sound of my mum's sewing machine, a quiet electric hum, and she spreads her paper dress patterns across the kitchen table. She buys *Vogue* patterns—I learn to say the word, "*Vogue*," which doesn't sound like it looks; it reads like a lumpy word, but when my mum says it, it is long and graceful, like the pictures of the ladies on the front of the *Vogue* pattern packets, their arms and legs poised like ballet dancers (and I want to be a ballet dancer when I grow up, I practice my ballet jumps in the kitchen, while my mum is sewing, I can nearly touch the ceiling, it's as if I can almost fly). My mum is so clever and so careful: she pins the paper patterns to her fabric, and cuts everything out in perfectly straight lines, and sews all the different shapes together to make a dress like the picture on the *Vogue* packet. She is as pretty as a picture (and one day a photographer comes, and takes our picture for a magazine. "Smile!" says the photographer. "Remember to smile!").

My mum's friend takes me shopping down the road in Regent's Street, to Liberty, which is her favorite department store; light and bustling, not like the Beatles' shop, there's no one lying around on the floor here. The baby is in a big pram, and I am helping push the pram, trying not to bump into the glass cases filled with sparkling jewelry (like the Crown Jewels, I think to myself, that we saw on a school trip to the Tower of London; like the Sleeping Beauty's abandoned tiara, left behind as she escaped from her glass coffin, on her way to liberty). My mum has already gone to Liberty to buy lengths of fabric to make new dresses for Ruth and me, and one for herself, which is greenish-brown, all covered in flowers, like water lilies, her long pale legs and arms just visible beneath. I think she looks very beautiful in the dress, but it doesn't seem to cheer my dad up. "It's too see-through," he says, "people will see everything." My mum shrugs, and says, "I don't understand what you're going on about"; and I don't understand either, I can't see what he means.

Anyway, my mum's friend says that she is going to cheer up

everyone today, in Liberty. She runs her fingers through rolls of cloth, all the different colors, running like water through her fingers. Her fingers are light, like the cloth, everything slipping and sliding and quickly, quickly, she has hidden something underneath the baby, in the pram. I look at her, but I do not say a word. "I'm going to make angel dresses," she says. "For the baby, you know, angel dresses, like this," and she spreads her arms wide, as if she were about to fly away, high above the glass cases, up to the roof, and through it, not splintering anything, just slipping free.

When we get home, my mother shakes her head. "You must stop this," she says to her friend. "You can't steal back what has been stolen from you." I'm trying to hang on to the edges of their conversation, not understanding, again, even though I know it is important; but it is broken into bits, dazzling yet incomplete, whichever way I turn it over inside my head.

Now, in another century, I think I'm beginning to piece it together, but not entirely, because it's someone else's story; someone else's broken marriage, impossible to patch up with stolen Liberty print lawn, translucent flowers spread thin; and the baby angel dresses are all gone (even if I knew where to look for them).

A little while ago, I was walking along Marylebone High Street, down the road from the golden angels who still watch over the parish, and the park beyond; and the door to where we used to live was open, and without thinking, I crossed the threshold, and went up the stairs, to the first floor; and there was another open door, to our old flat. Movers were shifting boxes toward the staircase, and a man in a suit, an American, was directing them. "Excuse me," I said, quickly, before I lost my nerve, "would you mind if I had a quick look? It's just I used to live here, a long time ago."

"Sure," said the American, "come in."

Inside, I found it hard to get my bearings, even though the flat was so small (just two bedrooms, how had all seven of us fit here?)—because it had been remodeled and reversed, so that the kitchen was now at the front, overlooking the High Street, and there was a bedroom in its place, at the back. But the middle bedroom I had shared with my sister, and the other kids, was still there, though it was empty, like the rest of the flat; and it seemed impossible, almost incomprehensible, that all trace of us had disappeared; that the Apple dress was not in the cupboard, that the dressing-up box was vanished, that everything, *everything*, was different now; that even in my memory, it would not, could not, be the same as it ever was.

And perhaps that's why we cling on to the smaller things that have somehow survived the years, against all the odds, when other stuff is lost: believing that a wedding ring (or a wedding dress) will remain one's own, in a way most other property does not. You could sell a wedding ring, of course, or throw it into the sea, or lose it when you were doing the washing up (as my mother did); but even if it did pass into another's hands, you could tell yourself it would not be remade in the way that a place you once lived might be. We pass through houses, and become their ghosts, like all the other people who ever lived within their walls, but most of us have a few bits and pieces that are ours, and ours alone, fixed like the colors of a stained-glass window; talismanic reminders of who we once were, and what we hope to become.

Not that I have my Apple dress: just a treasured photograph of me wearing it, one Halloween, with my sister next to me, and a jagged-toothed pumpkin on the table beside us, and scooped-out oranges filled with jelly. I wore that dress until I was bursting at its seams, until it fell apart, like a moth's chrysalis, discarded, but unforgotten.

You can never go back, of course. It's an impossible journey; as doomed as when you come across an old boyfriend, one you haven't seen for twenty years, and he says, "You haven't changed"; but you know you have changed, and so has he, and even if he kissed you, which he won't (he's married now, with children), you wouldn't wake up as a fairy tale princess in a dress made out of moonshine and a necklace of stars. Yet none of that stops you wanting to go back, very briefly; hoping for a temporary passport to the past (and, occasionally, the future, as well). It's what the White Queen tries to explain to Alice in *Through the Looking-Glass*—remembering backwards and forwards—though as the Queen admits, this "always makes one a little giddy at first."

But unlike Alice, I could not find the place I once lived in, when I returned there; and in revisiting it, I have muddled my memory. As for the orange Apple dress: I'd like to hold it in my hands again, for a little while, look into the mirrors, as if my past might be reflected there; as if the future might also be told.

4

School Uniform

IN THE AUTUMN of 1969, when the long summer had ended, we moved from London to Oxford, where my father had a new job as a university lecturer. It was a darkening time—my father became very depressed after the death of his mother, in December that year—but I remember a sunshine-y dress, a new school uniform, in blue and white cotton gingham, buttoned up the front, with a white collar. I liked the dress, but my sister loved it even more. She was still at infant school, but I had moved into the juniors: Bishop Kirk School, as safe and ordered a place as its name suggests. Not that there weren't ordinary accidents within its walls: one lunch-time, a bigger girl pushed me over in the playground and broke my two front teeth; another day, I took my knickers off by mistake, when we were changing for games, and a boy saw me, and told the teacher, but I was fierce by then and said that he was wrong, he had seen nothing, there was *nothing* to see, and he was the liar, not me.

Even so, most of the time, the school seemed as crisp and clear as my checked dress; not like home, where a volcano seemed to be erupting, where a sulfurous fog crept upon us, in between explosions and tremors that opened fissures all around. My father, the cleverest and most quick-witted of men, who had once been so swift and sure-footed, escaping from those who had wanted to imprison him in South Africa, was now held in the grip of something black and viscous and suffocating; though at times that which was leaden turned molten, so that he was tortured and boiling with rage. And there was no escaping his torment, not for him nor any of us, though one night I packed a small bag, and climbed out of a window onto the roof of the block of flats where we were living. When I was out there, I could see it was too high for me to jump down, and anyway, where was I to go, and what would become of my little sister if I were to run away?

Ruth was already feeling left behind, when I put on my gingham uniform in the morning. Sometimes she dressed herself in it, and I had to persuade her out of it, though at weekends and holidays, she insisted she be allowed to keep the uniform on. "It's not even a very nice dress," I told her, trying not to get cross.

"It is," she said. "It's a lovely dress. I want it, it's mine."

"It's not yours," I said, but eventually it was, and another one exactly like it, when she joined me at the junior school. We'd moved again by then, to a tall thin Victorian house in the center of Oxford, two rooms on each floor, and a back garden with espaliered pear trees along the old brick walls, and herbs growing within symmetrical triangles, the edges marked by miniature box hedges planted long before we'd arrived; but tended now by my mother, who was good at growing things (avocado plants, orange blossom and lemon trees, from the pips and seeds that others discarded). Ruth and I cycled together from the house to school, along Walton Street and up the Woodstock Road, faster and faster, set free for a while, wheels turning, the way ahead clear. We did not look back, though occasionally, I wondered which of the big houses on the Woodstock Road my mother's great-aunts had lived in, years ago, before I was born; before she'd arrived in England from South Africa. "I wish I knew the address," she'd say, almost to herself, "I'm sure I used to know their address." But the past was making itself manifest in other ways, by then, in the Victorian bottles that she unearthed in the garden, and then washed, carefully, and arranged on a shelf near the kitchen window, so that the sunshine lit up the green and blue glass. And was it the bottles that prompted her to set up a little antiques stall in the old cattle market? We'd go with her there at weekends, and help hang up the white Victorian nightdresses, camisoles, and christening robes that she'd washed and darned and ironed, having rescued them in jumble sales or job-lots in country auctions. Afterward, if it wasn't raining, she'd buy us Chinese food from the local take-out place, and we'd eat it in the park on the way home.

Then one day, at school, Ruth stopped eating; stopped talking, too. She would not say why, wept fat tears into her lunch. Who could blame her? Who could swallow that bitter-tasting liver, gray like the color of my father's face that morning? ("There's nothing for it," he'd said, "but for me to bring this house down.") My sister did not eat her lunch that day, or the next, kept her mouth shut for a week, until the headmaster, a kindly man named Mr. Appleton, called me into his study. "Is there anything wrong at home?" he said. "Anything the school should know about?"

"No," I said, smoothing the creases out of my cotton dress, examining the squared lines of gingham, as if it were a cryptic code that might be broken after sufficient time.

"Are you sure?" he said.

"Well, our auntie Lil died a little while ago," I said, which was true (and she had left her garnet earrings to my mother; little ruby-red drops, like tears of blood turned into jewels), though I knew that Lil's death was probably not the cause of my sister's tears, nor my father's. But it seemed enough of an answer to satisfy the headmaster.

And so it went on, the daily run of an ordinary life; school uniform neatly ironed and buttoned up, even when other things were coming undone at home; smashed glass and broken voices, but shush, it's time for homework and chocolate cookies, and remember, don't forget to pack your games kit for tomorrow morning. (We were good at games, both of us, Ruth at the high jump and me sprinting down the hurdle track; quicker than anyone who tried to catch us; fortunate children, blessed by good luck and long legs.)

Years later, when I was the same age as my parents had been in that uncertain time, and suddenly feeling my own balance to be precarious, I went shopping, and without thinking, bought myself a short blue cotton gingham dress. I wore it throughout a dangerous summer, and then gave it away. I did not want patterns to repeat themselves; feared that I was somehow tempting fate.

But it's not quite like that, is it? By which I mean, the patterns of the past are not formalized, nor imposed upon us, but all mixed up—the good and bad of it, the sweetness and the bitterness; my parents getting it wrong, and also getting it right; which is what we most of us do, most of the time (trying hard, as well as being trying). When I think of my father now, and of what he suffered during his breakdowns, of what it means when people refer to a disordered mind, the school-uniform dress always floats into my head; its machine-made lines, repeating themselves over and over again; perfectly measured; the very opposite of randomness and disaccord. I used to think, "Why my father? Why me?" but now that I am older than he was then, I have realized, at last, "Why not?" Because life isn't uniform, and if it were it would be shrunk to something preconceived, rigidly formulated. Which is not to say that a life need be shapeless, but it is, of necessity, uneven and messy and inconsistent (as I am; as muddled as what has gone before, and what will come to be). If I could, would I make it different for my own children: everything neat and crisp and full of certainty, in what is commonly known as "the greater scheme of things," whatever that might mean? Perhaps—but it wouldn't last; even were it not an impossibility. What child wants unfailing regularity; who would choose to wear a school uniform for an eternity? Who could wish for a life reduced that way?

Not my sister, that's for sure; though Heaven only knows what she wears now . . .

5

Plastic Trousers

"Clothes are our weapons, our challenges, our visible insults."
Angela Carter, "Notes for a Theory of Sixties Style"

FROM A DISTANCE, they looked like leather, but close up, they were plastic; not through and through, but a black shiny exterior, applied to something clothlike. I bought them in Camden Market in 1977: it was summertime, and I had just turned sixteen, and it felt like the world was turning with me.

I wore the black trousers a lot: to see the Sex Pistols and the Clash and the Stranglers and Ian Dury and the Jam and Elvis Costello and the Damned. I went to clubs like the Marquee because I had an older boyfriend who was living in central London; and also to concerts with my sister, at Top Rank in Cardiff, where we had moved the year before. Cardiff was a shock: not so much the city (though it was very different than London and Oxford, where we had spent most of our time until then), but everything that came with it. My parents had split up again, and my father had moved from Oxford to Cardiff some time previously, where he had been appointed to a job in the university; and then one day my mother told us that we were going to join him there, that they were "trying to make another go of it." I remember that phrase: it didn't seem to make sense, the going and the trying and everything. But anyway, that was where we were heading.

So. I started at a new school, a big rough one that looked to me like a cement factory, in the middle of a gray concrete council estate. We weren't living on the estate, but three or four miles away, in a beautiful but ramshackle old farmhouse, at the end of a long potholed lane. Most days, for several months after we'd arrived, an elderly Estonian builder came to work on the house, which had no conventional drainage. He drove there in a three-wheeled bubble car, and he was naked underneath his overalls. When I complained about the fact that he undid his overalls while he worked, so that his genitals were clearly visible—and erect, when my sister and I were around—he said, in tones of great outrage, that he needed the constant circulation of fresh air to keep himself fit and healthy and hygienic.

I didn't much like living in the farmhouse in the countryside, and I didn't fit in at the new school: which wasn't the school's fault, not anyone's fault, I just didn't know how to blend in. I had the wrong accent, the wrong clothes, the wrong every-thing. I was English, and I was posh (that's what most of my classmates said, not that I'd ever thought of myself like that), and when there were fights in the playground—girls ripping each other's earrings out, so that their earlobes were left torn and bloody; boys flashing switchblades, which I'd never seen before—I was terrified, though I tried hard to appear as nonchalant as everyone else. None of them were interested in punk—they listened to Status Quo and Mud, and they wore jeans with sharp creases ironed down the front, and Fred Perry shirts, and the boys had smoothly shaved suede-heads, and the girls had tight bubble perms—but they were much harder, far tougher, than anyone I'd met in a safety-pinned T-shirt at the Marquee. Eventually, I made friends with a girl in my year called Maureen, who liked the same music as I did, but then she moved to St. Albans. Ruth, meanwhile, had been sent to a different school, where she was equally unhappy; and all that I could do to help her was turn up in the playground one afternoon, and tell the girls who were bullying her that I would kill them if they didn't stop. Oddly, the threat worked.

Anyway, we had each other, and after a little while we both gave up on any attempt to emulate the prevailing teenage style (where female success was helped by blonde hair and large breasts; and while Ruth had the latter, I did not, and though I was fair, unlike her, I was by no means "bubbly," an adjective that was applied to more popular girls). So Ruth dyed her dark hair bright blue, and I colored mine a shocking shade of neon orange, and I bought the black plastic trousers, which seemed to make an immediate and definite improvement in my life.

Now that I come to think about it, they must have smelled horrible: you couldn't wash them properly (the label actually spelled it out: do not wash), so I'd just give them a quick dip in the sink; and after too many sweaty nights at Top Rank, the plastic began to peel, slightly, away from the cloth interior. Nevertheless, they were still holding together two years later, when I went to Cambridge, where they were much admired in my first week. "Leather trousers!" said a boy in his third year, who seemed astonishingly mature to me. "Cool!"

They weren't cool at all, of course, but rather hot and sticky. And obviously, they weren't leather (not even warm leatherette, which was the title of a song I was listening to at the time, by Grace Jones). It occurs to me now, in middle age, that like the trousers, my teenage rebellion was only a surface coating, easy to peel away to something more familiar: I mean, I didn't run away to join a punk band, or become a groupie or a junkie or anything else. I didn't even insist on writing a university dissertation on the lyrics of the Clash (unlike a more defiant friend of mine, who also had a black spider tattooed on his arm; now hidden beneath the dark suit and well-ironed shirt he wears to work). To be honest, I was happier getting lost in *The Waste Land*.

And I suppose that's the thing about having parents who were more rebellious than their teenage children: I could certainly never compete with my father the Marxist when it came to outrage. He was the one growing a greenhouse full of cannabis plants, which my mother burned down one day, sending a potent cloud of smoke over our house; and after he danced naked on the table at a party, my own potential social exploits, by comparison, could never be any other but tame. Thus a clear equation was formed: if my father was wild, it meant that I could not be—at least, it seemed that way to me. So, I had plastic trousers, but no multiple piercings or heroin; bright orange hair, but a level-headed disposition (well, most of the time, though not in matters of teenage romance, when my cheeks burned and my heart bounced up into my throat, and I yearned to be yearned for, for abandonment, without being abandoned). Now that I have a teenage son of my own, I realize that my parents, though unconventional in their approach, made rather a good job of seeing us through adolescence; certainly, my sister and I never had any reason to accuse them of being boring or dull.

The trousers came to a sticky end, inevitably: the seams rotted away from within, and though I sewed them up half a dozen times, by the end of my first year at Cambridge they were beyond repair; too ripped, even, to qualify as an homage to Sid Vicious. I didn't mourn them much: by then I was buying second-hand tea dresses and ball gowns (in which I probably looked more eccentric than stylish, trailing torn net behind me, and ragged crêpe de Chine; despite my conviction that I was emulating Vivienne Westwood in her championing of crinolines). But if I'd been more of an astute collector, I'd have preserved my Seditionaries T-shirts, saved up for out of my holiday wages as a waitress, bought from Malcolm Mc-Laren and Vivienne Westwood's Sex shop on the King's Road. Despite their slogans—"Too Fast to Live, Too Young to Die"; "Destroy"—you can see similar ones now, over twenty-five years later, preserved at the Metropolitan Museum in New York, or on eBay, selling for hundreds, sometimes thousands, of pounds; like the carefully hoarded rare ingredient of a precious alchemic recipe for youth.

The irony of this should be obvious, of course; unless you choose not to look at it through the veneer of irony (the patina and polish that is supposed to protect that which we cherish). Yet what strikes me now is not the absurdity of the embalming of anarchy and teenage defiance, but something else. Vivienne Westwood was born in 1941: she's only two years younger than my mother, and it seems to me that maybe there are other parallels to be drawn as well. Actually, that's wrong: parallels and straight lines can't be drawn in something as hazy as my family history (let alone someone else's history; someone like Vivienne Westwood, who has always displayed a sure grasp of the importance of deconstruction and reinvention). But it's as if she—more so than her then partner, Malcolm McLaren—was way ahead of the teenagers around her: more explosive, more unexpected, yet also more enduring in her subversive influence. And there is much to admire in that.

As for my parents: even now, they can surprise me; even now, I continue not to surprise them. A couple of years ago, I had a fierce argument with my father that seemed to erupt out of nowhere, but which must have been smoldering for years. "You're so reactionary," he said, "you always have been," a comment which enraged me. "I'm not!" I shouted, as angry as a fifteen-year-old; except I didn't shout when I was a teenager; it never seemed to be the right time. "You're a Tory!" he jeered. "You write for *Vogue*!" "There are Marxists who write for *Vogue*!" I said, irrationally. "Yeah, well you're not one of them," he replied.

Anyway, to return to the plastic trousers: if that is possible, given that they have long since passed the point of no return. They were not revolutionary—the rebellion they represented was that of the most transitory sort—nor seditious; but they served their purpose. I felt good, not bad, in them, while they lasted, and you can't ask your trousers for any more than that.

Cocking a Snook (How to, in Middle Age)

1. First things first. What is a snook? The *Oxford English Dictionary* describes it as "a derisive gesture consisting in placing the thumb against the nose and extending the fingers." According to an American Web site, www. word-detective.com, this is a gesture also known by the British as a "Queen Anne's Fan" (and no, I hadn't heard that before, either). As a child, when I first became aware of the phrase, I imagined a snook to be a sort of snood; thus, I thought, to cock a snook might mean a jaunty letting down of the hair; suggesting a kind of cheekiness.

2. I was wrong. A snook is not a snood. Even so, I think one might still hint at one's potential for cocking a snook, by sartorial means.

3. The display of a G-string above a pair of low-slung jeans does not, however, count as cocking a snook; not in my book, anyway.

4. Paint your toenails black or glittering emerald-green or the color of silvery moonshine: they're your toes, your prerogative.

5. Wear a marabou or swansdown tippet over your more sober evening dress. Or marabou anything; yes, I know it sounds absurd, but small absurdities can be heartening (though I'm not very keen on feathered earrings; and remember, also, not to be overpowered by your marabou accessory; you're in control here, after all).

6. Feel free to buy yourself a short trench coat in bright red cotton canvas or rose-pink suede (though preferably an affordable one, because bankruptcy is not liberating); or a capacious silvery-pewter-colored handbag, or a pair of gold snakeskin heels. You don't have to wear navy. (But I'd prefer it if the snakeskin was fake.)

7. If a man says to you, "Cheer up, love, it might never happen," tell him it has happened, and do not force yourself to smile. Smiling is not a duty, but a freedom. It's up to you now: you are liberated from the expectations and conformities of youth.

8. Which has to be as good a reason as any to avoid a Botox overdose. Who wants to look like an egg?

9. Flip-flops. I love flip-flops. Find the right pair, and I promise you, they are the easiest form of instant insouciance.

10. But not in winter. In winter you need boots. Mine are made for walking, but they have just enough of a tough wedge heel to let me hum Nancy Sinatra to myself, as I pass hooded teenage boys loitering in the park. ("One of these days these boots are gonna walk all over you . . .")

6

Ghost Dresses

"She looked beautiful in this velvet. Put it against your face. It's soft, isn't it? You can feel it, can't you? The scent is still fresh, isn't it? You could almost imagine she had only just taken it off. I would always know when she had been before me in a room. There would be a little whiff of her scent in the room. These are her underclothes, in this drawer. This pink set here she had never worn. She was wearing slacks of course and a shirt when she died. They were torn from her body in the water though. There was nothing on the body when it was found, all those weeks afterwards."

Daphne du Maurier, *Rebecca*

I

DO CLOTHES HAVE ghosts, or do ghosts have clothes? There's no evidence one way or the other, as you might expect: but there are stories, some of which survive long after their telling. I was talking about this, quite recently, to a friend of mine, Harriet Quick, the fashion features editor at *Vogue* (whose name, incidentally, has always seemed to me most fitting for her work, as a translator of rapidly shifting trends). We were having lunch together, and I asked her if she'd ever felt haunted by a piece of clothing, and she told me the following tale.

"There's a second-hand shop, around the corner from the football field on Fulham Road, and I used to go there quite often, on Saturdays, to hunt for stuff. And one day, I found a jet-beaded top that fell from the shoulders in butterfly sleeves, and fastened with minute black buttons from the waist to a gentle décolletage.

"The label in the top said 'Biba,' and I remembered my mother telling me about the Biba shop in the sixties, and how she used to sit me under the Victorian hat-stands that displayed the stock. Apparently I sat there and chewed shirttails, while she tried on the clothes. So when I slipped into the changing cubicle in the second-hand shop, and put on the black top, I had already opened a small peephole of memory. It took me a little while to fasten all those tiny buttons, and then I looked at myself in the mirror: but the face that stared back at me wasn't mine."

Harriet paused at this point in her monologue, and looked over at me, to check that I wasn't laughing at her. And I wasn't, because she was so serious; in fact, I felt the hairs standing up on the back of my neck; had that creeping sensation over my skin that Freud called "the Uncanny." "Go on," I said to Harriet. "What happened next?"

"Well, it sounds impossible, but in the mirror, instead of my reflection, there was a girl with flame-red hair and porcelain-pale skin. She had green eyes—I could see her eyes, but I don't think she could see me—and she was thin, terribly thin. And as I looked at her, she seemed to be falling, and I nearly fell, too, and beyond the mirror, I felt that she was swaying in a room in a white stuccoed London town house, filled with people jostling and screeching at each other."

As Harriet described the girl, I could not help but imagine

my slender redheaded mother, who wore Biba clothes and whose green eyes shone out of porcelain skin; but I knew that was another reflection in a different looking glass, that my mother's past should have no place in Harriet's story. "So what did you do?" I said to Harriet, who was now paler than usual, herself.

"I took the top off, straight away, but it was hard, because I was fumbling with all the buttons, but I wanted it off—I couldn't bear being inside it—because it felt funereal, like a shroud."

"As if someone had died in it?" I asked.

"Yes," said Harriet, "I felt sure that the girl in the mirror had been wearing it on the night she died. So I put the top back where I'd found it, and left the shop, feeling very shaken. And I tried not to think about it again—I didn't tell anyone, because it seemed so irrational—but I was just reading the diaries of [the fashion designer] Ossie Clark, and I came across an entry that describes an infamous party-girl with flame-red hair, who lived near the King's Road, and who died of an overdose."

"And you think it was her Biba top that you tried on?"

"Yes," said Harriet. "I think so."

II

Occasionally, lying sleepless in the dark, as it edges toward the dawn, I remember being frightened as a child in bed at night, about what might be hiding behind the closed wardrobe doors. I'm not scared anymore, but it is in those wakeful hours, when it feels as if everyone else is sleeping, that I sometimes think about other clothes in other ghost stories: of the profoundly disturbing scenes in Daphne du Maurier's *Rebecca*, in which the second Mrs. de Winter is haunted by her predecessor's clothes, almost from the moment she arrives as a young bride at Manderley with her new husband, and suddenly knows herself to be badly dressed ("in a tan-coloured stockinette frock, a small fur known as a stone-marten round my neck, and over all a shapeless mackintosh, far too big for me and dragging to my ankles"). But it is Rebecca's mackintosh that she wears on her first walk to the sea—to the place where Rebecca died—and Rebecca's lace-trimmed handkerchief that she finds in the coat pocket. "She who had worn the coat then was tall, slim, broader than me about the shoulders, for I had found it big and overlong, and the sleeves had come below my wrist. Some of the buttons were missing. She had not bothered then to do it up. She had thrown it over her shoulders like a cape, or worn it loose, hanging open, her hands deep in the pockets."

Rebecca's lipstick is still on the handkerchief, as is her scent, "like the crushed white petals of the azaleas" in the Manderley gardens. "I don't think much of people who just judge one by one's clothes," says the nameless second Mrs. de Winter, bravely, soon afterward, when she admits to her husband that she feels herself to be "dull and quiet and inexperienced." But clothes take a central part in the ensuing drama, as the means by which Rebecca's presence is felt: most palpably when the second Mrs. de Winter finds her way to Rebecca's bedroom, still kept as if in readiness for the dead woman's return, satin dressing gown on a chair and slippers beneath. "I picked up the slippers and held them in my hand. I was aware of a growing sense of horror, of horror turning to despair . . . On a sudden impulse I moved away from the bed and went back to the little ante-room where I had seen the wardrobes. I opened one of them. It was as I thought. The wardrobe was full of clothes. There were evening dresses here, I caught the shimmer of silver over the top of the white bags that enfolded them . . . There was a train of white satin, dripping on the floor of the wardrobe. Peeping out from a piece of tissue paper on a shelf above was an ostrich feather fan."

When the black-clad Mrs. Danvers follows the second Mrs. de Winter into Rebecca's bedroom, the horror increases. "I feel her everywhere," says the housekeeper (the keeper of Rebecca's wardrobe, of her memory, as well as Manderley). "You do too, don't you? . . . It's almost as though I catch the sound of her dress sweeping the stairs as she comes down to dinner . . . Do you think she can see us, talking to one another now? . . . Do you think the dead come back and watch the living?"

And it is the malevolent Mrs. Danvers (as haunted by Rebecca as this new bride) who persuades the second Mrs. de Winter that she should wear a copy of a white dress from a portrait of one of her husband's ancestors; not telling her that this was the same white dress that Rebecca had also had copied to wear to the last fancy-dress ball at Manderley. So that when the narrator appears before her husband in the white ball-gown, she looks like Rebecca reincarnated; and the suggestion that she is herself a ghost—more of a ghost than the dead woman into whose shoes she has stepped—is heightened, and finally voiced, by Mrs. Danvers, again, in a second encounter in Rebecca's bedroom. "Mrs. Danvers came close to me, she put her face near to mine. 'It's no use, is it?' she said. 'You'll never get the better of her. She's still mistress here, even if she is dead. She's the real Mrs. de Winter, not you. It's you that's the shadow and the ghost . . . Well, why don't you leave

Manderley to her? Why don't you go? . . . It's you that ought to be lying there in the church crypt, not her. It's you who ought to be dead, not Mrs. de Winter.'"

The second Mrs. de Winter survives Mrs. Danvers's attempt to—quite literally—push her over the edge into madness and suicide. ("Why don't you jump?" says Mrs. Danvers, as they stand before an open window in Rebecca's room. "Don't be afraid . . . You can jump of your own accord.") But even as the new bride lives on, Rebecca rises again, out of the sea, her body identifiable by the rings on her fingers; and in the final chapter, as the narrator falls asleep on a journey back to Manderley (a house engulfed in fire, in an echo of *Jane Eyre*), she dreams that she is possessed by Rebecca. "I got up and went to the looking glass. A face stared back at me that was not my own. It was very pale, very lovely, framed in a cloud of dark hair. The eyes narrowed and smiled. The lips parted. The face in the glass stared back at me and laughed."

Daphne du Maurier has often been described as someone who didn't care about clothes, in her characteristic uniform of shirt and trousers; and when I talked to her son, Kits Browning, about this, he said, "I couldn't imagine anyone less interested in clothes than Mum." But Kits's wife, Hacker Browning, disagreed. "Daphne had a passion for her shirts," she said, "and she was terribly particular about her trousers, which came from Jaeger. And she was besotted by belts—from Dunhill, from Hermès—if she had one, she had fifty. And she loved her perfumes, from Penhaligon and Yves Saint Laurent, and she had fortnightly appointments with her hairdresser. So contrary to what people say, Daphne was very concerned about her appearance." She also made the intriguing observation that Daphne's mother, Muriel—a former actress who had given up her career to nurture her husband, the actor Gerald du Maurier—might well have been the glamorous model for Rebecca's clothes: "Muriel was terribly grand, dress-wise, and in a way that Daphne wasn't." It is tempting, though probably fruitless, to speculate why the contents of Rebecca's wardrobe, like Muriel's, should be so much more ornate than Daphne's, or the second Mrs. de Winter's (and why Rebecca's beauty—still manifest in her surviving possessions—should be so threatening and sinister); but what is true is that clothes are not only a symptom of unease in du Maurier plots, but also of hauntings.

Thus in her short story "Don't Look Now"—written in 1970, over a decade after the death of Daphne's mother—a grieving mother is told by a blind psychic medium that her dead child lives on; the psychic offering proof, as they often do, in the precise description of an outfit, "even down to the little blue-and-white dress with the puff sleeves that she wore to her birthday party." (Recently, when I met a renowned Scottish medium named Gordon Smith—popularly known as the psychic barber—he told me that ghosts were simply memories, unlike spirits, which exist, without clothes or other material accoutrements, as pure energy; a distinction previously unknown to me. "So how come you sometimes describe a spirit in a particular outfit?" I said to Gordon, trying not to sound impolite. "That's just the way they show themselves," he said, "so that I can identify them to their grieving friends and relatives." Afterward, I thought of the popular Victorian mediums, some of whom found ways of swallowing and then regurgitating white muslin, or hiding swathes of it and then materializing ghostly shapes, which was named by them as ectoplasm, in a darkened room.)

"Don't Look Now" is famously unnerving, of course, like *Rebecca*; and anyone who knows it will shudder at the reminder of the other childlike figure in the story, a pixie-hood covering her murderous face. But there's another, lesser known, but equally sinister short story that I've read, "Hand in Glove" by Elizabeth Bowen, set in Edwardian Ireland, that describes two orphaned sisters living alone with their ailing widowed aunt, whose trousseau they ransack in the attic to remake as their own. After the old woman dies, due to their neglect, the older sister—ambitious to make a good marriage, and with her eye on a lord—breaks open the last of her aunt's trunks, only to be strangled by a white glove from the cache the sisters have coveted for so long.

Yet most disquieting of all, I think, are the ghosts in "The Turn of the Screw," because even if you have managed to convince yourself that they are figments of the governess's imagination, then how can she describe Peter Quint's clothes sufficiently accurately to convince the housekeeper that he has, indeed, risen from the dead? His ghost, reports the governess, who has never met Quint in his lifetime, is hatless, and dressed in "somebody's clothes. They're smart, but they're not his own." At this, Mrs. Grose, the housekeeper, "broke into a breathless, affirmative groan. 'They're the master's!'" she says, having listened to the governess. "'He never wore his hat, but he did wear—well there were waistcoats missed!'" (Interestingly, Henry James's governess, like the second Mrs. de Winter, is unnamed, unlike the ghosts in their narratives—Rebecca, Miss Jessel, Peter Quint—who begin to seem as real as their precisely observed clothes.)

"The Turn of the Screw," like the du Maurier stories, has never lost its power to shock me; yet for all that, the ghost dresses in my own life are not the frightening kind (nor could they be). Who wore the first Ghost dress, my sister, or me? My friend Polly lent me one of hers in 1995—sky-blue, with an embroidered bodice—to take on holiday to the Canary Islands, when my youngest son was still a baby. But I think it was Ruth who actually bought a Ghost dress of her own at the end of that year, when she was in the early stages of her pregnancy with twins: a pale bias-cut slip, cleverly cut, she pointed out, to skim over her body; and very practical, because it went in the washing machine, which justified the high price.

Ghost dresses were sold in the Ghost shop, which was just around the corner from Marylebone High Street. It's still there, actually, at number 14 Hinde Street, one of two Ghost stores in London, and a very good place to go to for a wedding dress. I mention this because so many women I know have been married in Ghost outfits; in fact, I almost convinced myself I'd worn one for my wedding in 1993; but when I checked just now, pulling it out of a box on the top shelf of our wardrobe, I discovered I was wrong, it was a linen dress from Nicole Farhi (pretty, but more easily crushed). And I thought the same about my sister's wedding dress—Ghost, it had to be, in another summer ceremony, in 1994. But actually, I was mistaken, again: I've looked at the photographs, and she was in Nicole Farhi white linen, like me; not the characteristic soft crêpe of all Ghost dresses; not the same thing at all.

A few true things (amid the mist and myth of my own making)—as told to me by Ghost's founder and owner, Tanya Sarne, when I interviewed her just after London Fashion Week, in September 2003. She started out in the fashion business in 1976, after her mother had died suddenly, and very unexpectedly, of pneumonia. "And now I often ask myself whether I'd have gone out and started my business, if my mother hadn't died," said Sarne (a woman almost as famous for her robust ability to survive in a tough industry as she is for her delicate-looking gossamer clothes). "While my mother was still alive, I was never on my own—she was always there to help—but her death made me very fierce, very angry, with a determination and an aggressiveness that I didn't have before." One might therefore assume that her mother was the ghost behind Ghost, but she says not; the label launched in 1983, after Sarne, by then a single parent of two children, had fallen out with an earlier business partner. "And one night I got drunk with Katherine Hamnett, and we came up with the name, and it struck me as a good one. My father had been a ghost-writer, and I thought I could hire designers, and have a kind of ghost-written collection. And then of course the fabric that we use—that we've always used, from the start—looks rather ghostly and ethereal."

One might question why it is that women want to look, if not like ghosts, exactly, then somehow wraithlike (it's a question of fragility, I suppose, of choosing to give an impression of otherworldliness; half Titania, half Ophelia). Except it didn't seem that way when my sister started buying lots of Ghost clothes after she was diagnosed with breast cancer; and it didn't feel that way when I bought some for her, as well, on shopping expeditions that took place after we'd met for tea and cakes in Sagne's Patisserie, a café just a few yards away from the block of flats where we'd lived, all those years previously, on Marylebone High Street. (Sometimes, as well as the cakes, we'd buy Sagne's marzipan pigs—our favorite treats when we were young—and then eat them on our way to the Ghost shop, instead of saving them for our children.) Of course, if you were being objective—which I am not—you might also ask why a woman with terminal cancer should want to wear the Ghost label; but it didn't seem possible that she would die, even though she was spending money like there was no tomorrow.

Anyway, one afternoon, after chocolate Florentines and her favorite Earl Grey tea, I bought my sister a black Ghost shirt and skirt; "The only way to disguise my stomach," she said, prodding at it mournfully. "I look pregnant, don't I?"

"No," I said, "you don't."

"I do," Ruth said, "except it's a tumor in my liver. Fucking cancer, it's so fucking expensive, having to buy a whole new wardrobe to accommodate it." She sounded angry and rueful and scathing and scared, all at once (which was happening a lot in our conversations then, as we veered between near-hysterical laughter and tears; trying to say everything, and also nothing at all). Then she pulled out a long gray-green dress from the racks, a narrow floor-length sheath. "Try it on," she told me, "you'll look lovely in this." So I did, and she was right, it was beautiful.

"I've got nowhere to wear it," I said.

"You can wear it anywhere," she said. "You can wear it on holiday or to parties. You could get up in the morning, and wear it to work. You can do whatever you want."

Now, when I remember this conversation—and I do remember it, vividly; unmuddled, sharp, unlike other fading memories—I wonder whether Ruth was trying to tell me something else, as well. Perhaps she was reminding me that I would go on living, even though she was going to die; that I would have other places to go to, and from, when she was contemplating a more lonely, unalterable journey; that I had choices, as she did not.

Perhaps that's what she was saying . . . But maybe she just liked the gray-green dress, a mermaid shade; the color of the sea.

When Ruth died, in the night, toward the end of an Indian summer, she was not wearing any of her Ghost clothes. Her dress was dark charcoal-gray jersey wool; the color of ashes, I could say, except she'd been fond of that dress, it was not quite as somber as it sounds. It was long, though not down to her ankles; and when she had come back to the hospice on a Sunday afternoon—having made her escape for the weekend, as she often tried to do—she had on black opaque tights beneath her dress, covering her frail wasting legs. Her husband, Matt, had taken their children home (they were tired, only two years old) and I stayed with her, though she was leaving, it seemed to me; too sick to want me to read to her, as I'd done in the weeks before, sitting beside her hospital bed; too far away to be comforted by her favorite story of brave-hearted Pippi Longstocking. First, she'd clawed at her tights, in pain, crying out loud, and I'd helped the nurses take them off; but then they gave her morphine, and she was peaceful, in her long dress, drifting, dreaming. My mother was there, too, as day turned to night, and she placed a soft filigree cashmere scarf at my sister's cheek; pale cobwebby gray, like the worn baby blanket Ruth had loved as a little girl; her comfort blanket, the one she'd never wanted to throw away.

Ruth had the scarf with her in the coffin; her body still in the charcoal dress; and then she was cremated, ashes to ashes, and floating away, like smoke, over the Sussex Downs, over the graveyard where we gathered, afterward, beneath a blue sky that stretched toward the sea.

I'm not sure what became of her Ghost dresses: my mother

kept some, I know, but I did not want those (though I have Ruth's favorite green mohair cardigan, folded among my sweaters in a drawer; and her black Gap jacket, which I still often wear, and it never seems to fade; resilient, resolutely material, in the most surprising way).

But when I dream of her, she is in her Ghost dresses; sometimes on a bicycle, tantalizingly close to me, yet also out of reach. It's like a mixed-up Chagall painting—a dream version, not the real thing; just as my dream sister is not the real one, either—a wedding-day bride on a bicycle, roses in her hair, white dress floating around her, guests and groom and everyone else on the ground beneath her, as the dream girl pedals higher, further, up above the roofs of the High Street; smiling and serene, while those below her raise imploring hands, entreating her to stay.

After her death, I did not go back to the Ghost shop for a very long time, and then at last, on a gray December morning, I persuaded myself that it would be a good idea to go to the warehouse sale. Not that it took place in a warehouse—it was in a large room, above a Victorian town hall and library (like another dream, it seemed)—and I went there alone, and picked out armfuls of clothes from the long racks. It was busy, and everyone else was talking, but I felt wrapped in silence, and wanted to leave, but then I thought I should try on a dress. It was black velvet, quite long—the same length as the dress my sister was cremated in—and as I looked at myself in the mirror, it was like looking at a ghost.

I started crying, but no one could see, there were no tears on my face, no sound coming out of my throat; I felt invisible, like a wraith lost in limbo.

The sensible thing would have been to go—to abandon the

velvet dress, and all the others, to get out into the un-fresh air outside, where London traffic streamed toward the Westway. But I didn't. I bought the black dress, and a couple of other things as well (palazzo pants, they're called; except palazzos are in short supply to use as a suitable backdrop).

I've worn the trousers subsequently, but never the velvet dress. It hangs in my wardrobe, accusingly, an unwrapped Christmas present for a ghost. As for the green-gray mermaid dress I bought on that last shopping expedition with my sister—it's vanished; where to, I have no idea, which is infuriating. And Ruth was right, I could have worn it anywhere, but now it's nowhere, stolen away: a loss which makes me feel a bit guilty, and angry with myself, as well, but mostly surprised, all of which are diluted versions of the emotions I feel about my sister's death. That should have been obvious, shouldn't it? But it took a lost Ghost dress to remind me of that; a mermaid dress, gone with my disappeared girl.

Ghost Footnote

After my sister died, I had a telephone conversation with the celebrated medium Rita Rogers (famous for having been consulted by Princess Diana, and also because of her work for the police in murder investigations). She did not know my surname—"I don't like having names and things," she said, "I don't want too much information from you"—but she came up with a list of names of my dead relatives: first Pat and Fred, Minnie and Louis and more, and then Ruth. While she was talking, I made notes in shorthand, automatically, like the journalist I am trained to be, even though I felt dazed by what she was saying about Ruth, didn't feel like a journalist any more. "She's very close to you," said Rita. "And she flutters around her children all the time. She adores those children. She says to you, be sure that they have good shoes."

Disappeared Clothes (A Familiar Lament)

1. My mother's Biba jersey minidress; pink-and-purple-striped, like a psychedelic bee; and her orange-and-scarlet-ribbed Biba sweater, both of which I loved.
2. The black Joseph trouser suit that I bought—and wore—to my sister's memorial service. (A mourning outfit that I do not mourn; it was like a carapace, while I was disappearing inside.)
3. My mother's wedding dress, as I have mentioned previously.
4. The brown linen Nicole Farhi trousers that I wore to my sister's wedding. They weren't that nice (elasticized waistband, to accommodate my postpartum belly) but even so . . .
5. Several hundred odd socks, inevitably.
6. The silver crocheted Lurex miniskirt my mother made especially for me; chewed up and unraveled by our escaped hamster, Hammy, beneath the floorboards of the Oxford house. At least I knew where the skirt had gone (we discovered his nest, several months after his bid for freedom, woven out of silvery threads and his other poached haul, my mother's half-made patchwork quilt).
7. But all the other lost clothes seem to have followed the socks, in a wrinkle through time. Perhaps they are being worn by our doppelgängers, in a parallel universe. (Not that the odd socks would be of much use there, either; unless it is a one-legged world.)

8. Could this be why, at this very moment, I'm feeling as if I haven't got a thing to wear? I do, in fact, have a well-stocked wardrobe; and the moment will pass. But I just don't like any of my clothes right now, tainted by the suspicion that there is a hole in the back of my wardrobe, where all the good things go.

7

The One That Got Away

"Fashion is not simply a matter of clothes; fashion is in the air, borne upon the wind . . ."

Coco Chanel

"A vague idea of birds; birds of vanity, like peacocks, parrots and swans."

Miuccia Prada, on the inspiration for her
spring/summer 2005 collection

"Ah, they put pigeons' feathers in the pillows—no wonder I couldn't die!"

Emily Brontë, *Wuthering Heights*

ON 21 SEPTEMBER 1998, a year (less a day) after my sister had died, I was in New York to interview the fashion designer Helmut Lang. I felt crumpled in every way; too messed up to meet a man then deemed the master of cool modernity. That morning, waiting to do the interview, I'd sat in my hotel room for a while, unable to face Manhattan (which was irrational, of course, given that the city had no interest in me). I watched the television: Bill Clinton's testimony to the grand jury about his affair with Monica Lewinsky was being broadcast to the American nation; the President looked uncomfortable in a dark suit, starched shirt, and tie. Sometimes he put on a pair of half-moon spectacles, which gave him a professorial air, as he debated the precise meaning of "sexual relations." None of it seemed to hang together, not from where I was sitting, on an uncomfortable white chair in a small white room at the Paramount Hotel. I did not like the Paramount: it was supposed to be a sleekly stylish container from which fashionable travelers could go forth each day (a role not unlike that which Lang's clothes were assumed to play); but it felt inadequate in the face of the messiness of the President's life, and mine.

So I gave up on the Paramount and the President, and walked to the Helmut Lang store in SoHo. In the window there was a single rack of dark clothes, as if it were an installation in a museum or gallery; further inside the store, a trio of vast black stone eagles watched over the proceedings, beside a column of flashing neon messages designed by the conceptual artist Jenny Holzer. The messages said: I AM CRYING HARD. THERE WAS BLOOD. NO ONE TOLD ME. NO ONE KNEW.

I tried not to catch the attention of a disapproving Germanic shop assistant. He was on the phone saying, "No, I can't help you, maybe you could ring back tomorrow morning." And then he rolled his eyes in my direction and said, "Ladies from Nebraska call me. They want to talk about fashion. They want to buy the clothes by mail order. They don't realize that not everyone can wear these clothes." I wasn't sure if I was included in the latter category, but I slunk past him and tried on a pair of trousers that I liked, and a cotton T-shirt: both of them creamy ivory; the trousers functional in shape, though not in color; the T-shirt soft and comforting, in a way that seemed surprising in this place. I bought them both, without

61

meeting any obvious resistance from the shop assistant, and then went downstairs, to Helmut Lang's office and showroom, to look at his latest collection, which would arrive in the shops the following January.

The T-shirt had softened me up a bit; but nevertheless, I was still in a mood to dismiss Helmut Lang's version of mono-chrome modernism as being as unsuitable for real life as the Paramount. And that's when I saw it, hanging on the rack: a white silken wool coat, which looked to me as if it had been made out of feathers. It came in other colors, too: black or palest beige or rose pink, but the white version was the one that I loved, because it reminded me of angel wings. (Not that I've ever encountered a real angel; though I imagine their wings would be properly feathered; wide enough, when opened, to cause a shadow to fall around them.) I wasn't sure whether anyone else would have seen the coat as being feathery—and it certainly wasn't explicitly angelic—but when I met Helmut Lang, shortly afterward, I mentioned this to him. "Angel wings!" he said, his face lighting up, in a way it had not done before (because Lang is a quietly serious man, an Austrian brought up in the mountains by his grandparents, after his parents divorced when he was three). "I try to slip something angelic into every season. Maybe wings, maybe just in the way a cape flows."

Lang was a man of few words, who did not trust the descriptions most often applied to his work. ("What does 'modern' mean?" he asked, and I was unable to provide a satisfactory answer, feeling then that my own grip upon the flow of time was shaky, as if life had turned in on itself, become more circular after my sister's death.) But despite the hesitan-cies of our conversation, he did express the same unexpected enthusiasm for the stone eagles that guarded his shop entrance as for the near-hidden angel references within the lines of his otherwise austere collection. "Before the birds were there," he said, "the building was beautiful, but it felt like it was missing something. Then I found the eagles, which came from an American embassy. I love the wings."

We said goodbye, and I did not ask him if I could buy the coat—it wasn't yet for sale; and even if it was, I knew I couldn't afford it (on a quick calculation from dollars to sterling, I reckoned it would cost at least £550). Apart from anything else, I'd already bought the top and the trousers, which looked more useful, *suitable*, in a way the coat did not.

Back in London, I kept thinking about its beautiful featheriness; but the coat was still somehow out of reach, even as the New Year approached, when I knew it would soon be flown across the Atlantic, to sell to British customers. At that time, when so much seemed unavailable to me (most of all my sister), I could not imagine myself owning the coat. I was not doing very much shopping at the time, except for food at supermarkets; though I am ashamed to say that I stole something on one of those expeditions—the only shoplifting I have ever done, before or since; a potato masher, the most prosaic of implements, the essence of usefulness, yet entirely unnecessary, given that we had a perfectly good one at home. (When I say shoplifting, it was not quite as active as that suggests: I put the potato masher in my cart, did not take it out again at the checkout, because I didn't really want it, and then wheeled the cart to the car, where I loaded the masher, along with the shopping, into the trunk; all of which would amount to guilt in the eyes of the law, of course; and an angel of justice, if any happened to be watching over me.)

So there I was, at the beginning of 1999, with two potato mashers, no angel coat, nor a sister. This might seem like an insane equation, I know, but nothing really added up for me then; the classical laws of the universe—of gravity, light, motion—seemed close to dissolving, as I was, or suspended and incomplete. As for the Helmut Lang trousers and T-shirt: they had both been inadvertently shrunk in the wash, and looked small enough to fit a baby.

Anyway, I decided to put the coat behind me; and resolved to move on, which is what people kept telling me to do. I'd already started a new job, as features editor of *Vogue* (I'm compressing things here, but speed, surely, is of the essence when one is attempting an escape); and I found it strangely soothing to be working in a place that concerned itself not only with the surfaces of things, but with the idea that reinvention was always close at hand; that transfiguration could be found in the rising and falling of hemlines; where the seasons of fashion (as marked on the catwalks of New York, London, Paris, and Milan) were as clearly delineated as the turning of the years. I did not steal any more kitchen implements, or anything else, for that matter. I did, however, buy a pair of feathered shoes from Russell & Bromley (rather similar to a far more expensive version by Gucci, a style much desired at the time): a pair of kitten-heeled mules, with a single strap across the arch of the foot trimmed with dark green, almost black, feathers. I loved these shoes above all others; and despite their seeming impracticality, they made me feel sure-footed, a little more able to navigate my way through the unknown territory that lay ahead, of an unmapped life with a disappeared sister who was not yet dead to me, nor ever could be. (And the feathered shoes reminded me, too, of what my father had called me, when I was little; what he sometimes calls me still: J-bird, he says, in his emails to me. Dearest J-bird, I hope you are well.)

Several years later, the shoes were not worn out, despite missing a few feathers; and I took them with me on a trip to Paris, where as part of a story I was doing for *Vogue*, I was given the opportunity to visit Lemarié, a couture workshop in rue du Faubourg Saint-Denis. One of five ateliers owned by Chanel (purchased in the 1990s, but all of them dating back to the nineteenth century, and famous for their exquisite craftsmanship), Lemarié specializes in feathers, providing them, in various gorgeous and decorative forms, to the couture houses. The atelier will have been refurbished by now, the spidery cracks in its walls filled and replastered, but when I went in the early summer of 2004, it remained largely unchanged since its establishment in 1880: an ancient wooden door leading from the street up several flights of stairs, past the tiny original kitchen where the feathers were still being cleaned and steamed, to the workshops, lined with wooden boxes and drawers, from floor to ceiling, each of them hand-labeled with nineteenth-century copperplate. Here, deep in the boxes, hidden under yellowing paper, were the most precious feathers, some from extinct birds, but preserved for decades in this place. "A feather can live forever," explained my guide, "as long as it is kept from the light." I asked her if I could open one of the drawers, the one marked "Birds of Paradise." Yes, she said, I could; though this was very precious, the last remainder of their irreplaceable stock. Inside the drawer, beneath its paper shroud, was a bird, its head still attached, its wings folded; far more macabre than I had expected; a reminder that this had once been a living thing (though feathers, like hair,

65

seem somehow not quite alive, even before their molting). And lying beneath that bird, there were others, too; all of them long dead: some of them a hundred years old, but the jewel-like blues and greens of their feathers iridescent in the dusty air of the atelier.

The birds in boxes were shocking things—their stillness the antithesis of a living bird trapped inside a room, beating its wings against the window glass, yet equally disturbing—and I was still staring at them in their wooden morgue when my guide closed the drawer, shutting away the sunlight. She motioned me to follow her into another room, where several women were sewing a long train of pale peachy-pink feathers. "*Vautours*," said one of the seamstresses; vulture feathers, dyed and trimmed and remade in a fairy-tale costume for a Hollywood princess. "Are there any feathers that people here see as bad luck?" I asked. There was a murmured conversation between the seamstresses, and some shrugs from my guide, and then she said, "Peacock feathers—a superstition shared by Mademoiselle Chanel herself, because they are the emblem of an evil eye."

Later, back in London, I tried to make sense of what I had seen, but without success. I thought of Hitchcock's terrifying film *The Birds* (based on an equally macabre Daphne du Maurier short story; though du Maurier hated the film), in which the impeccably dressed Tippi Hedren is turned from an elegant fashion-plate to a clawed and bandaged wreck. And I remembered, and reread, the characteristically violent episode in *Wuthering Heights*, when Cathy—believing that she is close to death, but not yet dying—tears open her pillow with her teeth, and identifies the feathers within it. ("And here is a moorcock's; and this—I should know it among a thousand—

it's a lapwing's . . . This feather was picked up from the heath, the bird was not shot—we saw its nest in the winter, full of little skeletons. Heathcliff set a trap over it, and the old ones dare not come.") Among them are the pigeon feathers that she says are keeping her from dying: a reference to the superstition that their presence on the bed will prevent the soul from leaving the body, if only for a little while. Other feather-obsessives may be interested that Iona Opie's *A Dictionary of Superstitions* confirms this, yet also refers to the belief that a pigeon, "especially if white, alighting on the house or flying in front of one indicates death." And John Updike's short story "Pigeon Feathers" has his central character, David, shooting the birds in a barn, feeling as he kills them like "a creator"; each bird a "dab of life, when he hit it, blossomed into a dead enemy." Afterward, when he gathers up the dead pigeons, he is astonished by the beauty of their feathers, "no two alike, designs executed, it seemed, in a controlled rapture, with a joy that hung level in the air above and behind him." Not that their beauty makes him mourn his actions; instead, "with a feminine, slipping sensation along his nerves that seemed to give the air hands, he was robed in this certainty: that the God who had lavished such craft upon these worthless birds would not destroy His whole Creation by refusing to let David live forever."

Actually, if you wanted to, you could construct an entire anthology of feathers—a sort of fluttering, impermanent birdcage; Flaubert's parrot pulling out his feathers in "A Simple Heart"; Lewis Carroll's shabby borogove, its feathers sticking out like a live mop; Zelda Fitzgerald's letter to her husband-to-be, Scott, thanking him for sending her a feathered fan ("those wonderful, wonderful feathers are the most beautiful things on earth"); and a later letter, begging him for a parrot for Christmas, after her nervous breakdown. (In the meantime, she had a borrowed parrot, and observed its "long senseless conversations in the exact inflections of people transacting very serious business. It's curious how they employ very exactly and aptly the tone of the human voice to fit their feelings, and have no sense of the words they use at all . . . I *must* have one.") For several weeks after my trip to the Paris atelier, I began collecting more of these feathery excerpts—all of which were prefaced, in my mind, at least, by Emily Dickinson's poem ("Hope is the thing with feathers / That perches in the soul / And sings the tune without the words / And never stops at all").

But none of what I'd read had helped; there was no consolation in it, I wasn't feeling hopeful, I was feeling confused. I fretted about the fate of a green parrot that had swooped daily over our garden in north London, a wonderful sight that I'd taken to be a good omen when we moved house the previous summer; but it had disappeared the following winter, to join a flock not far away on Hampstead Heath, I liked to think; though on dark days, I worried that it had been captured by the same people who caged dozens of birds in the shadowed backyard of a local pub, their song drowned out by the noise of MTV from inside the bar. (I contemplated the possibility of tracking down a cell of animal-rights activists, to set the caged birds free, but aside from the primary difficulty of finding a team of avian liberationists, I became more hesitant after someone told me that there was a plan to cull the Hampstead flock of wild parrots, as not being indigenous to north London.) I was also increasingly preoccupied by the story of a female swan whose mate had been killed by a dog on the

Hampstead ponds; the swan and her cygnets were still alive, but she seemed very alone, to me, as she swam around in circles. ("Swans are not, in fact, necessarily monogamous," said a more cheerful friend of mine whose garden overlooked the pond. "She may find another mate." But I wasn't convinced.) When I took our dog for her daily walks around the local park (a waterless place, with no swans in it, though the parrot had lived there, briefly), I wondered if the feathers on the ground—white feathers, like a trail—were a message; but I decided this was a sign only of my own uncertainty, a looking for meaning when there was none. Occasionally, downy pearl-gray feathers blew through the open back door into our kitchen. "Angel feathers," said Tom, my youngest son, and I wanted to believe him; but then I'd remember the dead birds in that wooden drawer in Paris.

Writing this down now (on a computer, not with feather quill and ink; I'm not *that* obsessed), I'd like to be able to make a joke about it—because I realize it must sound laughable, parrots and pigeons and Emily Brontë, all mixed up in an inedible feathery soup. But I can't yet find the joke: in fact, just about the only thing to emerge from this gloomy confusion is the continuing link, in my head, at least, between feathers and death, as well as angels and the afterlife. For if feathers are signs of hope, then the gathering and capturing of them is also a reminder of how far we will go in the pursuit of our desire; killing in order to make our own winged creations. (In *Killing the God*, the second volume of Sir James Frazer's *The Golden Bough*, Frazer described the American Indian tribe that worshiped the buzzard, and killed the divine bird each year, after which it was mourned, and its feathers preserved to be used as ceremonial garments. "They believed that though they sacrificed the bird annually," Frazer wrote, in a passage drawn upon by Freud in his work *Totem and Taboo*, "she came to life again and returned to her home in the mountains . . . [They] were firm in the opinion that the birds sacrificed were but one and the same female.")

And none of this can be called useful or practical; not that practicality is necessarily the best armor against neediness or grief or longing—those are the things that call for feathered wings. That's probably why I, as a child, like so many other little girls, had fallen in love with *Swan Lake*; practiced ballet, endlessly, inelegantly, in the dream that I might one day wear the feathered costume of the beautiful, doomed swan maidens. And sometimes, even now, occasionally, I still dream of *Swan Lake*, a tunnel of sleep leading to a hidden doorway into an unnamed wonderland, where I am able to leap, effortlessly, arthritic knees vanished in the night, to fly like the Swan Queen, before she drowned. (I was talking about that recently, to the swanlike British model Erin O'Connor, who studied ballet for ten years, from the age of five, first as a cure recommended by a doctor for bow legs, then because it made her feel beautiful, when nothing else in life did, as a skinny six-foot teenager. And I'd also told her that I liked the picture of her in the December 2004 issue of *Vogue*, wearing a feathery Alexander McQueen couture gown, which had reminded me of *Swan Lake*. "The Mother Goose picture," she said, half-smiling. "I'm twenty-seven, and for the first time in my career, I sometimes feel self-conscious, having to go out on the catwalk with girls who are over a decade younger than me.")

Which brings me back to the coat. It's six years, now, since I first saw it: six years to the day as I write this now. Tomorrow will be the seventh anniversary of my sister's death, and I still haven't seen an angel (not that I'm saying the two events should be somehow linked; it's just that I'm aware that time is moving on, with or without me; that an otherworldly manifestation may never make itself visible to me, however much I might hope for a blessing such as this). A little while ago, I was talking to Harriet Quick at *Vogue*, and I asked her if she remembered the coat; not because I thought it would have meant anything in particular to her, but because she's the sort of fashion enthusiast who can recall the details of most collections. "Yes," she said, "and you know what, I ordered one in blush pink."

"You bought that coat?" I said, surprised, because in my head no one owned the coat, it just sort of floated from the catwalk into the ether. "Can I see it?"

"I'm afraid not," said Harriet. "It looked so beautiful when I got it, with that downy feather finish, but it turned into a mangy albino-dog coat after I'd spent too long standing in a taxi queue in the rain. I suppose it just wasn't meant for the elements . . ."

Oddly enough, I did not feel disillusioned by this. I was relieved, actually, that I wouldn't see the coat again, all these years later; and glad that it had always remained just out of my reach. It made me realize, too, that even if clothes do not have ghosts, the discarded, deadened feather coat lives on, still beautiful, somewhere, at least in my imagination; and I wonder if my sister might see it, wherever she is; though I try not to hold on to the thought of her; try to let go of her, as we are supposed to do; try to set her spirit free, like an uncaged bird, like the lost bird of paradise, or the green parrot, flying high above and beyond me, further and further away.

8

The Gap

> "To fill a Gap
> Insert the Thing that caused it—
> Block it up
> With Other—and 'twill yawn the more—
> You cannot solder an Abyss
> With Air."
>
> Emily Dickinson, poem 546

> "Hearts may fail, and Strength outwear, and Purpose turn
>   to Loathing,
> But the everyday affair of business, meals, and clothing,
> Builds a bulkhead 'twixt Despair and the Edge of Nothing."
>
> Rudyard Kipling, "The Supports
> (Song of the Waiting Seraphs)"

I

I'M NOT QUITE sure why The Gap became, simply, Gap; or to be more specific, I know the official reason—that it was a branding exercise, which took place in 1989—but I don't know what the point was of losing the definite article (a sort of gesture to comfortable informality, perhaps, in keeping with Gap clothes?). Anyway, as far as I was concerned, it stayed

The Gap for years after the rebranding: I didn't even notice that I was supposed to have noticed a change. I just kept on buying my jeans and T-shirts there.

In fact, I seemed to be sleepwalking through the Gap global invasion. I didn't know that the first Gap store had been set up by Donald and Doris Fisher in San Francisco in 1969 (I only know that now because I've just looked it up on the Gap Inc. Web site). I couldn't have told you that its first international outpost was in London in 1987. I was dimly aware that it had been targeted by the anti-globalization campaigns that were gathering force by the late nineties; but I didn't know whether or not its store windows had been broken in the May Day riots in London in 2001. To be honest, The Gap was still a gap in my consciousness; which is shameful, I admit, but I'm trying to be honest here.

As for the clothes: well, I liked them, but I didn't love them. They filled the gap between functionality and fashion; they did the job they were designed to do. I bought my first pair of Gap jeans from a sale rack soon after my first child was born in 1989: I couldn't fit back into my much-loved frayed and faded Levi's, but the new ones were fine. Actually, they were more than fine—they were kinder to the female form than the narrowly cut Levi's, which I'd bought long before pregnancy, when I still had a more boyish shape—but I didn't really notice that; I was just getting by, in a blur of sleeplessness and post-natal hormones (which in my case, turned everything into a calm sludge).

It wasn't until eight years later—a period in which I continued to shop regularly at Gap, for children's clothes, as well as for my husband and me—that I felt more than a passing attachment to the label, attributed something more to it than simple usefulness. My sister had just died: and those who have lost someone they love, whether through betrayal, bereavement, sacrifice or schism, will probably recognize that there is a "before" and "after" that attaches itself to the loss; a clearly delineated mark, as recognizable as any physical scar. After that breaking point, the gap that Ruth left was not filled by the Gap jacket that she left to me; and it wasn't as if she bequeathed me her black jacket in a will, or anything like that; I'm not sure we ever discussed it. But she had worn the jacket regularly, for several years at least (a Prada nylon lookalike, it was remarkable for its robust staying power; almost as appealing, like the best Gap designs continue to be, as its luxury label counterparts)—and in the first days after her death, when her husband, Matt, was going through the contents of her wardrobe, there seemed to be an unspoken assumption that the jacket would go home with me.

Matt also gave me one of her favorite rings—a silver band, made of three strands, that was slightly too big for any of my fingers, so I threaded it through a fine-link chain, and kept it around my neck. Which might sound a bit albatross-like; but it wasn't. I found it comforting, looping it round in circles, when I was trying to think (and trying not to think, as well).

Eventually, though, I stopped wearing Ruth's ring around my neck. I hung it on the chain on a hook above the mantelpiece in my bedroom, next to a posy of dried lavender; and when we moved house, nearly six years after Ruth's death, I put the ring away into a small jewelry box, in safekeeping for her daughter, Lola.

But the jacket is different: I still wear it throughout the year, unless it is very hot (for even in midwinter it provides good protection against the elements); and the strange thing is, it never seems to date or age. Its only mark of the passage of time is a cuff button, which must have fallen off before Ruth got ill, and which she sewed on again; and I can see, now, that the black thread she used is slightly different from the original (her thread has faded over the years, to a sort of rusty brown).

When I think about my sister's jacket, it seems inexplicable that it should have survived, while she has not. Or, to be more precise—because Ruth *has* survived, in that I still love her—what is surprising is that the jacket remains as material evidence of her life, when her flesh and blood is ashes. Her body filled this jacket; now it does not. (Just after she died, when I was still working for a newspaper where long hours were seen as the sign of commitment and success, I noticed that certain colleagues always left a jacket hanging on the back of their office chairs after they had departed for the night, as a reminder that they would return, that some essential part of them had not, in fact, gone. At the time, I was hoping that my sister might make her presence manifest, that her spirit would materialize, however briefly; for it felt impossible—improbable—that she was never coming back; though it didn't occur to me that she would do so through the means of her jacket, which was clearly abandoned by her, cast off in the way that my colleagues' suit jackets were not.)

You might think that the gap represented by the Gap jacket—the void, or veil, between the living and the dead—is a gap too far, so deep, so entirely complete, that it seems absurd to hang on to this small reminder of my sister. And you could be right; but the thing is . . . *the thing is* . . . the black jacket is this thing, this immutable object. It has not given up the ghost. It does not contain her, but the fact that it once did provides some useful containment for me.

I also happen to like the jacket. It's a good look, as a *Vogue* fashion editor once said to me, as she admired it in the lift at work. "It's only the Gap," I said, and then, for a few seconds, felt surprisingly treacherous.

II

I know that I'm not alone in recognizing that clothes can, if not bridge the gap between the living and the dead, then provide (as Kipling observed) a bulkhead between despair and the edge of nothing. This doesn't always work—you need only remember those horrific pictures of piles of shoes, collected together in heaps after those who had worn them had been gassed in Nazi concentration camps—but sometimes, in smaller ways, in less extreme moments of history, the bulkhead holds.

You can see it in the collected letters of F. Scott and Zelda Fitzgerald (a couple hailed as the brightest of the Bright Young Things, but whose marriage was lived in the shadows of her mental illness and his alcoholism). The letters are compelling in many different ways—their sophistication and charm all the more seductive for the acknowledgment that they were teetering on the edge of the Crash. When I first read them, having already fallen in love with Scott Fitzgerald's novels as a teenager, I didn't consciously associate Zelda's breakdowns with my father's, but now I can see that part of what made her letters so absorbing to me must have been because they seemed to provide clues to my father (and also the suggestion that in madness, there might also be clarity; that the distance between sanity and insanity was not so great, after all). In particular, Zelda's frequent references to clothes are a reminder, among other things, of how fiercely she fought to keep herself in the everyday world, even when she was in and out of mental hospitals, when sanity seemed just beyond her grasp, and doctors were also jailers; when the gap between herself and her husband was widening, and she saw him, too, as the instigator of her incarceration, in places where straitjackets replaced party dresses, and her dancing feet were stilled.

As it happens, it was Zelda's dancing—in the form of a period of intense ballet training, undertaken in the hope of becoming a professional ballerina—that was identified, rightly or wrongly, as one of the catalysts for her first breakdown, in 1930, when she was admitted to a psychiatric clinic on Lake Geneva. While she was there, the Fitzgeralds wrote two long letters of reminiscence to each other; Zelda's reads almost like a tormented Mrs. Dalloway, except that her stream of consciousness is given some order with memories of clothes. "There were my white knickers that startled the Connecticut hills, and the swim in the sandaled lady's bird-pool . . . I had a pink dress that floated and a very theatrical silver one . . . There was Paris and the heat and the ice-cream that did not melt and buying clothes . . ." But the references to clothes are more than punctuation of the slip-sliding narrative of her life— toward the end of her letter, when she describes the frantic dancing, and the crisis her ballet training precipitates, she pinpoints it thus: "I couldn't go into stores to buy clothes and my emotions became blindly involved." It would be entirely wrong, I'm sure, to suggest that it was her inability to buy clothes that presaged the breakdown; but even so, clothes become a kind of shorthand—as well as a reality—for the ability to be well put together; to appear rational, rather than blindly emotional; to make one's way through the world.

Without the containment of clothes, the world began to come apart for her; as she wrote in another letter to Scott, also from the Swiss clinic, "colors were infinite, part of the air, and not restricted by the lines that encompassed them and lines were free of the masses they held." And then she, too, felt herself come apart, first with "a detachment as if I was on the other side of a black gauze—a fearless small feeling . . . But even that was better than the childish, vacillating shell that I am now. I am so afraid that when you come and find there is nothing left but disorder and vacuum that you will be horror-struck."

Scott's letter to Zelda, written soon after she entered the Swiss clinic (a draft which may never have been sent), also speaks of the unhappiness that had preceded her mental collapse. "You were going crazy and calling it genius," he wrote, "I was going to ruin and calling it anything that came to hand." But in attempting to be more precise in his description of the gulf that had opened up between them, he described her at home, as "a phantom washing clothes" (a perplexing phrase; though perhaps Scott felt his wife to be a ghostly domestic presence, when he realized the extent of her desire to be set free).

There were recriminations in these letters, but later their separation was more peaceful. "Do you still smell of pencils and sometimes of tweed?" wrote Zelda in a letter to her husband in the autumn of 1930. And in December, she asked him to send her "some books of your choosing—and for a present I want a silver ring for my little finger—a heavy masculine kind with a red stone—ruby or garnet or something like that. Clothes I need desperately but I'll get them in the spring when things are brighter and less hopeless than just now . . ."

The following spring, she was allowed to leave the clinic for day outings—"Darling—I went to Geneva all by myself with a fellow maniac"—and told Scott that she was missing him terribly: "Have you ever been so lonely that you felt eternally guilty—as if you'd left off part of your clothes—I love you so, and being without you is like having gone off and left the gas-heater burning, or locked the baby in the clothes-bin." (It's hard to imagine a better description of the explosive anxiety that made a powder keg out of their marriage; the same sort of anxiety that can displace itself from human relationships to clothes. Thus instead of recognizing that we feel out of sorts, or out of love, or out of our depth, we feel out of fashion, instead.)

Zelda's daughter, Scottie, was ten in 1931; no longer a baby, old enough now to visit Zelda in the clinic (who had, in fact, been the one locked away in a bin); but still young enough for toys. ("Dear Love—I've made Scottie some wonderful paper-dolls, you and me and her, but they have no clothes yet . . ." And later, when Zelda did make the paper clothes, the otherwise conventional outfit, made for her papery self, was winged.) By the autumn of 1931, Zelda was sufficiently recovered to leave the Swiss clinic and return to her hometown of Montgomery, Alabama, where the Fitzgeralds moved into a house close to her parents. But money was tight, as usual, and there was another separation, when Scott went to Hollywood to work on a screenplay (the film was *Red-Headed Woman*, starring Jean Harlow, though Fitzgerald was fired before it went into production). Zelda wrote in a letter to him, "I feel very poor . . . I'd like to put on my old clothes and dig a field." Two sentences on, she said, "I think of you and want to live in a velvet riding habit and recite Swinburne and be a ghost in every crumbling brick house on the country roads." And soon afterward, as Christmas approached, she wrote: "Your closet is full of lovely silver packages. It looks so sad to see your clothes getting dusty on their hangers . . . if you come back . . . I will let you play with my pistol and you can win every golf game and I will make you a new suit from a blue hydrangea bush and shoes from pecan-shells and I'll sew you a belt from leaves like maps of the world and you can always be the one that's perfect."

As difficult as it is to know the truth of the Fitzgeralds' marriage (did his drinking send her crazy, or did her craziness send him to drink?), it is also too easy to turn Zelda into a perfectly imperfect mythic figure—a fantastical, semi-fictional creation, like the glamorous heroines of her husband's novels. But that would be to ignore her real determination and discipline: the desire to not be closeted away; to bridge that gap between herself and her husband; between madness and sanity, craziness and creativity, promise and failure; between being in the world, and being out of it. (Interestingly, the idea that physical beauty, like beautiful clothes, might lead one back into the confines of the wardrobe, imprisoned rather than liberated, is also apparent in her letters; in November 1931, she wrote to Scott, "I will be very happy that you are so handsome and when I see how handsome you are my stomach will fill with many unpleasant emotions like a cake with too many raisins and I will want to shut you up in a closet like a dress too beautiful to wear.")

And always, always, she continued to note down the concrete details of dress: even in February 1932, when she was hospitalized again, at a psychiatric clinic in Baltimore: "Dearest—It seemed very sad to see you going off in your new shoes alone. Little human vanities are somehow the most moving poignant things in people you love . . . I didn't finish your socks. It seems awful that you should be doing them again . . ."

And so it went on. Zelda's novel, *Save Me the Waltz* (based, in part, on their marriage, as was her husband's masterpiece, *Tender Is the Night*), came out in October 1932, but received harsh reviews and did not sell well. (There is a vivid episode in it when the heroine is invited as a soloist to Naples by a ballet company there, just as Zelda herself had been; in reality, she did not accept the invitation, though in the novel the heroine does go to Naples, as the prima ballerina in *Swan Lake*; though afterward her foot becomes infected, which ensures that she will never dance again.) The couple had argued over which of them had the right to use the shared autobiographical material in their respective novels; but their lives were increasingly divergent, both from one another, and from the stylish models for the Jazz Age that they had been held to be. Scott was still drinking too much; Zelda hated his drinking; nevertheless, she left the psychiatric clinic and moved back in with him and their daughter, to a rented house just outside Baltimore, which was badly damaged by a blaze started after Zelda burned some of her old clothes in the fireplace of an upstairs room. (It is not clear what precipitated that conflagration in June 1933; but six years previously, when Scott had become infatuated with a young Hollywood actress—an affair fictionalized in *Tender Is the Night*—Zelda had responded by setting fire to her clothes in a hotel bathtub.)

By March 1934, when Zelda was in a different psychiatric clinic, this one on the Hudson River, north of New York, she wired Scott asking him to make sure that all her clothes were sent; a trunk duly arrived, though as was made clear in a subsequent letter, she had more detailed requirements: "I would also like my blue bathing-suit which may be in the box with moth balls in the back room on the third floor, and also the rest of my clothes: a blue suit, a green checked skirt and the evening clothes." Zelda's precision about her wardrobe is intriguing, given that her thinking had been characterized by others, including her husband and doctors, as disturbed and chaotic (and in moments when I have felt spiraling despair, I have found an odd comfort in rereading those descriptions, and the implication that order might be restored with the packing and unpacking of clothes).

Two years later, while Scott struggled with alcoholism and depression, Zelda had been moved to the Highland Hospital, in Asheville, North Carolina. By then, she was experiencing religious manias, and there were times when she would dress only in white, and insisted on dropping to her knees and praying when visitors arrived. Scott, writing to friends, said, "Outside of the realm of what you called Zelda's 'terribly dangerous secret thoughts' I was her great reality, often the only liaison agent who could make the world tangible to her."

And yet, as Zelda's letters constantly reveal, she did not give up on her own attempts to make the world tangible to herself. She painted pictures, some of which were admired and exhibited, and she continued to make marvelous paper dolls and clothe them with paper clothes. "Thank you for the check," she wrote to Scott from the Highland Hospital in August 1936. "Last year I spun enough cloth to smother Clotho [one of the three Fates in Greek mythology, the spinner of the thread of human life] and to disgust forever the three fates with their trade—So I'll have it made into a nice Poiret suit or something indespensably [*sic*] useless enough to contribute to a sense of great luxury."

The following month, thanking Scott for more money, she wrote, "I think I'll buy one presentable suit in case the house catches on fire and I have to help work the hose." When, finally, the Highland Hospital caught fire, on March 10, 1948, Zelda died in the flames (imprisoned in the attic, according to some accounts, like Bertha Mason in *Jane Eyre*). Her body was so badly burned that it could only be identified by her slipper, which was found lying beneath her corpse.

By then, Scott was long gone, too; though Zelda had carried on writing to her husband, and he to her, until his death in Hollywood in December 1940. Their letters were tender, despite their years apart, despite disappointment, despite everything. Not long before Scott died, she wrote to him that a "lady is making me a deep-horizon blue suit." I like to think of Zelda in that blue suit, wearing the color of far horizons even in her locked hospital room; narrowing the gap between herself and a distant place, where the sea meets the sky; a place you can never arrive at, the very edge of everything.

9

The Velvet Jacket

"What do you weave from all these threads, for I know you
haven't been idle the while I've been speaking to you, bring it
nearer the window, and I will see, it's all wrong unless it has
one gold thread in it, a long, big shining fibre which hides the
others—and which will fade away into Heaven while you hold
it, and from there come back to me."

> Letter from Emily Dickinson to Jane Humphrey,
> Richard B. Sewall, *The Life of Emily Dickinson*

FOR MANY YEARS, ever since I'd started wearing it, at the age of
twenty or so, I believed that the black velvet jacket had
belonged to my Jewish past: in part because it looked as if
it might have done; high-collared, in a Prussian cut, its gold
embroidery threaded in an intricate pattern that I'd interpreted
as Eastern European (loops and flowers and leaves and whorls,
thousands and thousands of tiny stitches forming circles that
turn into ornate stars and pyramids). I was sure that my father
had told me its story: a sole surviving piece of material
evidence from long ago and far away; brought by my grandmother's mother as she made the journey from East Prussia to
Lithuania, to London and then South Africa. The fact that my
father knew so little about his mother's mother made her
velvet jacket all the more precious to me: her name was Rosa,

he said, and she was born in a town called Memel in East Prussia. She'd married a man from Vilna (now Vilnius, in Lithuania), my father's maternal grandfather; his name was Philip Moses Sacks, and they'd had three daughters: Minna (known to everyone as Minnie), my grandmother, who was born in Vilna in 1905; Anne, born five years later, after their arrival in South Africa; and Sarah, the youngest child, born in 1915.

My father didn't know Rosa's maiden name; he remembered her only as an old woman, after her husband's death, living with him and his parents in Johannesburg. "She was suffering from senile dementia by then," he told me, "and she used to repeat the same two stories from her childhood—the first one was about how she'd been dressed up in her best clothes as a little girl in Memel, when she was chosen to present a petition on behalf of the local Jewish community to the King of Prussia, asking him to be more merciful, to release the Jews from whatever oppression they were suffering at the time. And there was another story, which always made her giggle, about how she'd gone swimming naked in the river." My father said that no one could understand why those were the only episodes she remembered, over and over again: though now they seem to me to have a kind of logic, about being dressed up, and undressed, about the ruling grip of authority giving way to a moment of pure freedom. I wanted to know more, of course, but he couldn't add any details about Rosa's life ("Jewish families didn't talk about the past," he said, "or at least, mine never did"); and she died long before I was born. Even so, I imagined her clearly enough: a shrewd and resourceful woman; that's how she looks in the only picture I have of her, sturdy in a dark suit, jacket buttoned up, skirt reaching down to her ankles, to reveal a pair of flat Mary Jane shoes. In this photograph, her husband is standing next to her, his face more obscured than hers, by the shadow of his trilby, his suit a paler blur. Philip Sacks, according to his grandson, my father, was said to have been an unsuccessful businessman, running first a dairy in Balmoral, a mining town west of Johannesburg, and then working as a bookkeeper in the 1940s and '50s; but Rosa had made sure the daughters were well educated, sending them to a convent school in Balmoral. The family never had any money, and Minnie had provided extra income from the age of sixteen, teaching piano lessons; but somehow Minnie and Anne—both of them gifted musicians—had won scholarships to study at the Royal Academy of Music in London, and it seemed obvious to me that the velvet jacket would have been taken with them, on that long sea journey back to Europe. (Where had they lived in London? My father doesn't know the street, Bayswater, he thinks, but sometimes, as I pass the Royal Academy of Music, in Marylebone Road, I imagine that I might catch a glimpse of them whisking past, just ahead of me, the years between us caught up in a curve of time, looping in a treble clef. They are in dark suits and sensible shoes, like their mother, but at home—a rented room; a fog-bound street—the velvet jacket hangs in a small wardrobe, taken out on high days and holidays, its fine gold thread as precious as the chance that brought them to this cold place.)

How it had ended up in my mother's wardrobe, I wasn't sure. I guessed that Minnie might have brought it with her when she came to visit us in 1964, when my sister was born. I remember very little of my Jewish grandmother, except my hand in hers, the softness of her powdered cheek, a wordlessness that was not uncomforting. She did not look like the kind of woman to wear an embroidered velvet jacket; after the brief opulence of her wedding picture, she appeared only in dark coats and hats, an umbrella usually in one hand, protection against the elements (which makes her sound severe, but she was not; there was a sweetness about Minnie that remains even now, in the black and white photograph I have of her, on a mantelpiece beside me, as I write).

Eventually, a little while ago, I asked my mother when Minnie had given her the jacket.

"She didn't," said my mother.

"So did Louis give it to you, after Minnie died?" I said.

"No," said my mother, "it wasn't hers. It was my cousin Ann's—Auntie Lil's daughter. It was Lil who gave it to me after Ann was killed in a car crash."

As I've mentioned before, my mother has always retained her capacity to surprise me: not that she hides anything, but you have to know the right questions to ask. For some reason, I found this more unexpected than anything else she had said for a long time. I knew about Ann; knew the briefest of details of her death, at twenty-two, in a car crash a few days before her wedding (her fiancé had survived, as had the man who was driving the car). But why had I never known that the velvet jacket—which I wore to parties for many years, as I grew older, as Ann had never done—belonged to my mother's beautiful dead cousin? And she was beautiful, famously so: a model in South Africa, and, according to family legend, for *Vogue*, when she had come to live in London in 1954.

Unfortunately, my mother couldn't tell me much about the jacket, other than a vague idea that it was Yemenite, not Prussian, and a gift from Ann's fiancé; but she suggested I ring her cousin, Ann's older brother, Graham Knox, an architect who lives in Wiltshire, to ask him if he remembered more. He didn't; but we started talking, and more of Ann's story emerged. She had come to England at the age of twenty-one to pursue her modeling career, having made a big success of it in South Africa; Graham had arrived in London the previous year, 1953, to finish his architectural qualifications. Ann was already engaged to be married to another South African, Robin Halse (a marvelously dashing young man, my mother had said, educated at Cambridge and with a pilot's license, bold enough to have flown a light airplane all the way from South Africa to England). The wedding was set for June 1955; Lil arrived a few months before that, though the plan was that she and Ann and Robin were to return to South Africa after the wedding (Robin's family owned a large estate in the Eastern Cape, and he was going to take over the running of it). "I remember the dates so clearly," said Graham to me. "On June 17, 1955, just a few days before the wedding, Ann and Robin were due to come back to London, after a holiday in Cornwall and Scotland. But early that evening, for some reason, they took a detour to see a friend in Aylesbury. This friend took them out for a drive in his car—Robin was in the passenger seat, and Ann in the back, I think—and there was an accident—a headlong collision with an oncoming car. Mum and I had already gone to bed in our flat in London, and at 11:30 there was a knock at the door. Two policemen were standing there—and they told us that the boys were in hospital, but Ann had been killed instantly."

Graham was composed as he talked, but then his voice cracked, very slightly. "She was so beautiful," he said. "It still seems impossible, even now . . ."

Afterward, I decided to go and have a look in the *Vogue* archives, to see if I could find a photograph of Ann: because Graham had told me that he didn't have any of her as a model, and most of his family albums were packed away in a box in the attic. My mother has only two remaining pictures of Ann— as an astonishingly pretty little girl, blonde hair and perfect features, in a smocked print frock with her mother and brother; and then another, dated January 1954, eighteen months before her death, with her hair cut short, looking like a lovely teenager on the verge of adulthood—but I was intent on finding another photograph, proof of her brief time in London, so I made an appointment to visit the basement library at Vogue House, to search through the iron shelves of bound volumes of old magazines. But when I got there, I discovered an immediate obstacle to my plan: models were not named in *Vogue* unless they were well-known members of the English upper classes; and without any caption information, I had no real way of recognizing my mother's cousin. I kept turning the pages, though, hoping that I'd find a clue; and when no clues revealed themselves, I was still absorbed by the old magazines (for here, after all, were the antecedents of the *Vogue* that has employed me; that provided an unlikely sanctuary, after my sister's death).

For a moment, I thought I might have found Ann—the same curve of the lips; the same cheekbones, the same smile—but then I realized, I must be wrong, because it's a face that appeared again in a later magazine, October 1954, and it belonged to Miss Tilly Laycock, "daughter of Major-General Sir Robert and Lady Laycock." Her father was the new Governor of Malta, and Tilly had been photographed by Cecil Beaton in "a green and oatmeal speckled tweed dress with a channel of green suede; with it, amusingly designed gilt jewelry, a tan calf bag, cream chamois leather gloves." In the following issue, I found myself rather taken with the Duchess of Newcastle, "an expert horsewoman and enthusiastic motorist," photographed with her daughters, and wearing a splendid Worth ball gown, in cream satin embroidered with pearl and diamante, and a blue and green shot-silk stole. Meanwhile, declared *Vogue*, in one of its then-characteristic lists, "People are talking about . . . Mr Bevan's future plans, after Gaitskell's dramatic triumph at Scarborough . . . The expansion of the word 'co-existence' that now means so much."

Vogue is designed to be a diverting magazine, and I took the diversion it offered, kept turning the pages, way past those that might have offered a glimpse of Ann, until I reached the autumn of 1960, when my mother would have been shopping for her black wedding dress, and *Vogue* reported on the first major London store to have been built since the war ("Phoenix-like, the new John Lewis building has risen on the bombed-out site of its former Oxford Street premises") and Balenciaga princess coats and blonde-tweed suits from Dior. I examined the picture captions for the prices, which revealed that this was a time when you could buy a black cocktail dress in the finest worsted wool for nine and a half guineas: less than a fifth of the price my mother had paid for hers. So I was feeling quite surprised, again—and impressed by her, too—and the morning had turned into late afternoon, and I'd been sitting in the basement all day, and the library was about to close, but I'd just reached the issue announcing the *Vogue* Talent competition in January 1982, which I entered when I was still at Cambridge. (Entrants had to write their autobiography in 750 words or less.)

I already knew what happened next, even without reading it (which was just as well, because the librarians were hovering, time for everyone to go home): I won a prize, and was invited to lunch at Vogue House, and afterward offered a job, as a fashion features assistant, for an annual salary of just about £2,000, which wasn't really enough to live on in London, even in those long-ago days; no more than my student grant. I didn't take the job, but I did start writing for *Vogue*, periodically; and eventually, I returned to the magazine full-time, as features editor (a job I left when I was halfway through my first book, though I remain attached to the magazine, as a contributing editor, and in other, less distinct forms, as well).

All of which I was thinking about as I caught the tube home. I couldn't find Ann—and it's possible that I never will, in those un-indexed archives—but maybe I was also excavating in the basement for evidence of myself, of how I came to be there; and how *Vogue* came to mean so much to me. My mother had bought the magazine regularly when I was growing up—not every month, if money was short, though there was always a copy in the house, passed on from a well-groomed friend—and like the *Vogue* patterns that she used to make her clothes, and ours, it seemed redolent of glamour and sophistication: a blueprint for a better life.

But I also had the sense, too, that there was part of her which had grown to disapprove of *Vogue*: the radical part, that took her to Greenham Common as an anti-nuclear protestor in the early eighties: and she was the real thing, not a day-tripper, but one of the women who moved there and set up camp, in a homemade tepee, and who was jailed for her beliefs. Obviously, by the time she was in Holloway prison—which was just for a fortnight, but horrible and grueling for her, nevertheless—*Vogue* was not on her agenda; and I did not do anything as inflammatory as discussing my first job offer from the magazine, when I visited her, during her incarceration.

I know this sounds oddly illogical, but thinking about Ann's death—about how everything ended for her, so suddenly—also reminds me of my mother; not simply because they had been so close as children (my mother, the younger one, filled with admiration for her beautiful older cousin, who seemed to be the sister she never had; another girl, in an extended family of rugby-playing boys). When was it that my mother stopped caring very much about clothes, stopped buying *Vogue* patterns, put her sewing machine away? I think it might have been when I was a teenager; certainly, that was when she gave me her wedding dress, and the black velvet jacket, and the garnet drop earrings she had inherited from Auntie Lil; and by the time she went to Greenham, when I was at university, she seemed to have set aside the exuberant colors I remembered from earlier days (the purple Biba knits, an emerald-green cotton kaftan). Not that she'd given up altogether on making things: my mother had taken to knitting by then—beautifully made sweaters and scarves—and like some of the other protestors at Greenham she wove intricate rainbow woolen cobwebs around the chain-mail fence that separated the peace camp from the army on the other side. (When I visited her there, and saw her new home, a bivouac of branches and green leaves, I felt like an intruder; for although she and her companions were on the outside of the fence, they seemed to me to be on the inside of an invisible circle of their own.) I say she wove cobwebs, but hers were more abstract than that: rather like the patterns that cover the black velvet jacket; patterns that you could read anything into, though your interpretation of their meaning might be incorrect; or make sense only to you, and you alone.

Anyway, I'm straying a long way from the point—or rather, from Ann's jacket; but sometimes clothes can do that to you ("a jacket that takes you places": it's a phrase I've read—possibly written—in *Vogue* before . . .). This is a jacket without a label, like a book cover without an author's name, designed for an anonymous tale. It looks to me as if it was hand-sewn, embroidered as a one-off, wherever it came from—which may be one of the reasons why I've tried to label it for myself; incorrectly, as it turns out. It wasn't my Jewish grandmother's; nor is it a direct link to my mother (there's something about it that seems to get in the way between us; perhaps because it reminds her of those others she has loved, and lost; perhaps because it reminds me of all the things I don't understand). All I know, really, is that it belonged to a girl I never met, who died before I was born, whose picture I cannot find in *Vogue*.

I couldn't find Ann anywhere else, either: typing her name into Google unlocked no doors on the Internet, or at least, not the right ones; but then I tried another name in the search engine, her fiancé, Robin Halse; and much to my surprise, there was a phone number and address, in South Africa: still in the same family estate that he and Ann were supposed to return to, in married life.

I went to the phone, and dialed the number, before I had time to think better of it. A woman answered the phone: I asked for Robin, explained that I was calling from London. "I'm Robin's daughter," she said, "my name is Ann."

She gave me another number for her father, and I rang it, and he picked up the phone straight away, and picked up my story, too, even though I was faltering, shame-faced to have disturbed him in this unexpected manner, nearly half a century after the accident. I apologized, but he was immensely courteous, and said he was glad I had got in touch; he had found himself thinking about Ann recently, going over what happened, how it happened, the terrible event. "It's been on my conscience," he said.

"But you've nothing to feel guilty about," I said, surprised, "it wasn't your fault, you weren't even driving the car."

"I know that," he said, "but afterward, when I got out of hospital, I went back to South Africa . . . I didn't see enough of Ann's family, and I feel bad about that. But the whole thing was too dreadful for words . . ."

I told him that my family always spoke warmly of him—which is true, my mother has said how much Lil adored him—and that they felt no sense of betrayal, only the anguished loss that he was suffering. And then I remembered something else, my mother telling me that when Robin married, a long time afterward, he had raised a memorial stone to Ann on the estate; that he had sent a photograph of it to Lil and Graham. I said this to him, and his voice in reply was so close, it felt as if he was in the room with me, not six thousand miles away, on the other side of the world. "We were so sure we would be coming back here after the wedding," he said, "sure with all the certainty of youth."

I told him that I had Ann's black velvet jacket—that her mother gave it to my mother, and my mother gave it to me, and I shall give it to my sister's daughter, when I feel the time has come. He didn't remember it, not really, he said, though the details might come back to him. "That's OK," I said. "I'm just happy that we talked."

"I'm pleased, too," he said. "It means a great deal to me to have a conversation like this, when you reach my age."

I liked him immensely, this man who might have married my mother's favorite cousin; who still feels somehow related to me, if only in that he saw—and held—the girl in the black velvet jacket. The jacket doesn't matter, not to him, though it is precious to me, still. What matters is that they loved each other, and also, that he went on living, that his life went on.

Even so, I'd be lying if I didn't admit to having wanted a clear story to emerge out of the jacket: not the half-imaginary fragments that I told myself; because I wanted to find Ann, to discover her and make her real again. But there is no straight-forward narrative here: and perhaps that is the point. Some-times a piece of clothing can tell a story; sometimes we have to make up the story for ourselves.

Unfinished Business

1. I've always been partial to a raw-edged seam—otherwise known as selvage. It's rougher than a fringe, less finished than a frill; quite often used as a device by Miuccia Prada or Karl Lagerfeld at Chanel, though you can also find it in chain-store T-shirts.

2. My mother kept unfinished clothes: very occasionally, she'd start a dress, cut out the fabric and pin it, but never complete the task. She'd put it away in a drawer, like a half-written story. I always wondered what endings she had planned in her head.

3. There is something similarly unfinished about the clothes that F. Scott Fitzgerald dresses his heroines in; something that always leaves me wanting more. Like his description

of Nicole toward the end of *Tender Is the Night*, as she prepares to leave her husband: "She put on the first ankle-length day dress that she had owned for many years and crossed herself reverently with Chanel Sixteen." And? What color is her dress? What material? (Surely Zelda Fitzgerald would have told us these things?) Maybe he saw it as a mark of his masculinity to leave out the details of the dress; a gesture to Zelda, who accused him (in his words) of being "a fairy."

4. Virginia Woolf was far better at the details when she wrote about clothes, though one outfit—a hat and a dress, bought on the advice of her friend Dorothy Todd, then editor of British *Vogue*—remains mysterious; and its story incomplete. In her diary entry for 30 June 1926, she wrote: "This is the last day of June and finds me in black despair because Clive laughed at my new hat, Vita pitied me, & I sank to the depths of gloom . . . Clive suddenly said, or bawled rather, what an astonishing hat you're wearing! Then he asked where I got it. I pretended a mystery, tried to change the talk, was not allowed, & they pulled me down between them, like a hare; I never felt more humiliated." Todd is named in this diary entry as being responsible for the much-mocked hat and dress, but nothing more emerges, apart from the writer's anguish: "I came away deeply chagrined, as unhappy as I have been these last ten years; & revolved it in sleep and dreams all night; & today has been ruined."

10

The Return of the Little Black Dress

"It was a warm evening, nearly summer, and she wore a slim cool black dress, black sandals, a pearl choker . . . there was a consequential good taste in the plainness of her clothes, the blues and grays and lack of luster that made her, herself, shine so."

Truman Capote, *Breakfast at Tiffany's*

IT'S CURIOUS, the trouble you can have with a little black dress, when it's the very thing that is supposed to simplify your life. Get the dress right, so the theory goes, and it's as useful as a man's tuxedo or a well-cut suit: elegant, yet also functional; timeless, without being boring. But like Coco Chanel, who popularized the style in the 1920s, the little black dress is not necessarily as straightforward as we might expect it to be. Chanel made it look that way, of course: a supremely comfortable version of the chemise, designed to be worn without corsets, but with insouciance. By 1926, American *Vogue* had dubbed it "the Ford of fashion": speedy and easy and able to take you everywhere; a set of characteristics that we are still primed to look for—hope for—in a little black dress today.

That chic raciness was what attracted my mother, I suppose, when she chose a little black wedding dress; and it is her dress, the ur-dress, which sent me, without quite realizing why, on a haphazard search for one of my own. (Actually, there is one, partial, answer to the question "Why black?" It's flattering; or at least, it feels that way, which is why I keep coming back to it, like so many other women do, despite sporadic expeditions into color—though I'm not a fan of the funereal, all-black wardrobe.) The first I bought in Paris, sometime in the mid-eighties, which was round about the time my mother's wedding dress had been spirited away. It was black stretch jersey wool—a cheekily direct copy of Azzedine Alaïa, who was just about the most influential designer in the world at the time—and very cleverly cut, despite its modest price tag (long-sleeved, a couple of inches above the knee, fitted and flattering in all the right places, but as easy to pull on as a sweater, and completely unadorned). I wore that dress for years—to parties and offices and job interviews; with high heels and flat pumps—and my friends borrowed it as well (one attributed the start of several passionate affairs to its considerable charm; though it never had quite such a volcanic effect on my love life, unfortunately). Anyway, having held its own for so long, the dress finally, suddenly, went baggy in the early nineties, sagging beyond the point of no return; and it took me a while to find the right replacement. Eventually, at the end of that decade, I found it in a Chanel sample sale: knee-length, close-cut, but not too tight, with a black chiffon trim at the hem and neckline, to add a bit of frivolity to an otherwise somber wool crêpe; and over five years later, the dress still *works*; which is why I always turn to it, unlike other, more flamboyant affairs.

But it doesn't solve everything, however much I'd like it to. Recently, I was invited to a party held by the photographer Mario Testino at Kensington Palace, to celebrate the publication of his book of photographs, *Women to Women: Posi-*

tively Speaking, to raise awareness of women living with HIV and AIDS. That's exactly the sort of event where the little black dress is supposed to come into its own: from the moment you take it out of the wardrobe, you don't have to worry about what to wear, or how to wear it, and are therefore entirely free to concentrate on infinitely more important things. But the thing is, the trick didn't work, for once; I wasn't sure about the little black dress—just before I put it on, I remembered a photograph I'd seen of myself wearing it to the last fashion party I'd been invited to, and I looked horrible: sort of pasty-faced; moon-like, not chic at all. Which wasn't the dress's fault, but mine, and my age—and then I fell into a deeper slough of self-loathing, because what on earth was I doing, thinking about my stupid fat face and my stupid dress, instead of the terrible suffering of others, far less privileged than me?

It's a similar impulse that has made it so hard to write about the little black dress now: I keep starting and stopping, and deleting and rewriting; uncomfortably aware that the semiotics of a little black dress can seem grotesque in its irrelevance. And that's one of the problems of attaching importance to any particular fashion, as well as fashion in general: it's easily swept away, by weightier matters (and also by other bits of fluff, as well).

But for all that, I don't ever entirely give up on fashion, or the little black dress, which occasionally seems to offer itself up as an answer, even when I'm not sure of the question. Of course, the dress is insufficient protection against life's uncertainties and anxieties and tragedies; even Holly Golightly's perfect little black dress in *Breakfast at Tiffany's* doesn't keep her safe from the loss of her brother, or contain and disarm the rising dread that she calls "the mean reds." It's not the same as the blues, she says, trying to explain that dread: "No, the blues are because you're getting fat or maybe it's been raining too long. You're sad, that's all. But the mean reds are horrible. You're afraid and you sweat like hell, but you don't know what you're afraid of. Except something bad is going to happen. Only you don't know what it is." Holly Golightly's solution to the mean reds is to jump in a taxi and go to Tiffany's, not necessarily to buy anything, but just to be there: "It calms me down right away, the quietness and the proud look of it," a description that might as easily be applied to her little black dress.

Which brings me back to Coco Chanel, the prime proponent of the little black dress, its quietness and the proud look of it; who kept her faith in fashion, believed in its structures and strictures, in its power to endure, even when she said she did not. In fact, what she said—at least, in public, in the form of her famous maxims—was as carefully designed and reworked as her clothes (often by her friend, and former lover, the poet Pierre Reverdy, who would tactfully correct or complete the apparently spontaneous aphorisms that she jotted down). "Fashion should slip out of your hands," she declared. "The very idea of protecting the seasonal arts is childish. One should not bother to protect that which dies the minute it is born." And yet she protected and preserved her own designs—never letting them slip out of her hands, but returning over and over again to her talismanic iconography, the double C's and number fives; the camellias and pearls and little black dresses; the latter a version of the nun-like clothes she had been made to wear at the convent orphanage where her father left her, after her mother died; a blasphemous version, yet later taking on a holiness of its own in her hermetically sealed world.

The impulse—or at least, my impulse—is to want to break that seal, to unpick the seams of Chanel's little black dresses; to uncover what might lie beneath. If my mother's black dress still obscures the shadowy figure of who, exactly, she was on her wedding day (a former convent-school girl, among other things), then Coco Chanel is even more remote; impossible to grasp. Which is why I have found myself returning to Chanel, over and over again, exasperated and fascinated and always kept at bay (though how could I ever hope to understand her history, when I don't understand my own?). If you want facts about her life, there are very few—she refused to discuss her childhood, lopped a decade off her life with the same alacrity as she chopped hemlines and shortened dresses. But for all her attempts at covering up the circumstances of her beginnings, a certificate exists to show that she was born in Saumur on 19 August 1883, the illegitimate daughter of Jeanne Devolle, a shopgirl, and Albert Chanel, a peddler and merchant. She was named Gabrielle; she had a sister, Julia, and possibly several other siblings, whom she never discussed in later life; she was equally reticent about the circumstances in which her father abandoned his daughters in an Aubazine orphanage, the week after their mother died. At eighteen, Gabrielle left the orphanage, and moved as a charity pupil to a boarding school run by canonesses in Moulins; she stayed there until she was twenty, when she was found a job as a clerk in a hosiery shop. It was in Moulins that she became the mistress of a wealthy young cavalry officer, Etienne Balsan; and there, too, that she made her debut as Coco Chanel, singing at the local concert hall, with a repertoire of only two songs ("Ko Ko Ri Ko" and "Qui qu'a vu Coco").

Coco wanted to be a famous singer, but was more admired

for the hats and dresses that she made for herself and her friends; and in 1909, she set up a small business in Balsan's ground-floor bachelor flat in Paris. By the end of the following year, she had moved on to an apartment in rue Cambon (the street where the Chanel headquarters still are, today), having fallen in love with a friend of Balsan's, an equally wealthy man called Arthur ("Boy") Capel. It was Capel who provided her with the financial backing to open her first boutique, in Deauville in 1913 (the seaside resort where he played polo); by 1916, she had established herself as a couturier, and her innovations—bobbed hair, no corsets, tanned skin, shorter skirts—were sweeping Europe.

From then on, her story becomes legend; the events are true, or at least most of them are, but they have been told so often that it's hard to read between the lines. She had more affairs—with the Russian émigré Grand Duke Dmitri Pavlovitch and the Duke of Westminster, among others; and friendships with Cocteau, Diaghilev, Dalí, Man Ray. And there were more successes, including her launch in 1920 of the perfume that was to make her fortune, Chanel No. 5; and her endorsement by *Vogue* in 1926, when the magazine predicted that the Chanel little black dress—a sheath in crêpe de Chine with long, closely fitting sleeves—would become a uniform for all women of taste.

Somewhere along the way, the girl who reinvented herself from peddler's daughter to self-made businesswoman, who championed freedom and the right to define herself in whichever way she chose, turned into an implacable, immoveable icon. Several years ago, in Paris, after interviewing Karl Lagerfeld (the man who in 1982 replaced the dead woman still known at the Chanel headquarters as Mademoiselle

Herself), I was taken on a tour of Coco's private apartment above her shops and studio at rue Cambon, all preserved as she wanted; as if in amber, or like a mausoleum. We walked through the first-floor salon, where very rich couture clients gather to view the latest garments (or "pieces," as in pieces of art), toward the same mirrored stairwell, unchanged since Chanel's death in 1971; the white treads freshly painted every morning, "just as Mademoiselle Chanel ordered," explained my guide.

And then we walked up the staircase, the place where Chanel perched, like a magpie, during the seasonal shows, watching her audience through a sequence of mirrors while remaining hidden from their eyes. (Those who transgressed her rules, by talking instead of concentrating on the beauty of her pieces, were banished forever after.) At the top of the stairs was her apartment, kept pristine and hidden from the light, behind closed curtains. "Mademoiselle bought this building in the twenties and renovated everything before she moved here in 1935," said my guide, in a hushed voice, opening the curtains a little, but with a nervous look over her shoulder, as if a formidable ghost might upbraid her for disobedience. "You will see the characteristic Chanel colors—white, black and beige. The beige is in memory of the earth of the Auvergne, where she was born. And the black and white is in memory of the Aubazine convent where she was educated for ten years."

We admired the lacquered eighteenth-century Chinese screens and the ornate mirrors and the fortune-telling cards on a side table, still waiting to tell the future of a dead woman. "All the objects have a special significance," continued my guide, gesturing toward wooden carvings placed around the drawing room. "The camellias represent purity and longevity

103

and the bunches of wheat represent abundance and riches. Mademoiselle Chanel, as you know, came from a poor childhood, so she put this wheat everywhere to protect her. She was very superstitious.

"Look," said the guide, pointing out the chandeliers with their crystal drops in the shape of number fives; and the paired objects that mirrored each other across the room (two masks, two pillars, two statues of reindeer, frozen in front of the empty fireplace). "Everything was in pairs," explained the guide, "because she was sorry to be alone." She paused, and then glanced over her shoulder again (could Mademoiselle still be listening, watching, on the other side of the mirror?). And then she went on, even quieter than before. "Mademoiselle wanted to be married, but she never accepted the domination of a man. She became the Duke of Westminster's lover in 1925, but the relationship ended ten years later. He wanted to marry her, but she said, "No, there have been many duchesses of Westminster, but only one Coco Chanel!" She didn't want to tarnish the name.' (What my guide didn't say was that Coco herself tarnished her name, during the Nazi occupation of Paris, when she took as her lover a German officer, Hans Gunther von Dincklage. She had closed her salon when war was declared, unlike other couturiers such as Jeanne Lanvin and Jacques Fath, who continued to show their collections, but did not emerge unscathed after war had ended. According to Edmonde-Charles Roux, the author of *Chanel and Her World* and a former editor of French *Vogue*, "It was in the dark atmosphere of summary executions and kangaroo courts that Chanel was apprehended in September of 1944. Many years later she would still all but choke with fury when recalling the day two men arrived at the Ritz and unceremoniously demanded that she follow them forthwith. The order for her arrest came from the Committee of Public Morals. One can imagine the alarm that ran through her entourage. But a few hours later Chanel was released and allowed to return to the Ritz." Shortly afterward, she left for Switzerland, where she lived for the next eight years; though on one of her brief return trips to Paris, in 1948, she was photographed by the young Richard Avedon, then working for *Harper's Bazaar*. He asked her to pose in front of a wall; behind her, presumably unknown to Chanel, was a poster bearing the words "pourquoi Hitler." There Chanel leaned, cigarette in hand, in her trademark strings of pearls and, yes, a little black dress.)

"By the end of her life," said my guide, "she was lonely, but too old, too difficult, to change." I sat down on the same beige suede sofa that Chanel had described as being at the center of the world, feeling suddenly tired in this airless place, and the guide flinched at my impudence. On the coffee table in front of me were two crystal balls, and I leaned closer, to look at them, but could see nothing within, only the distorted reflections of lions. There were lions everywhere in the room: stone and wooden, like the amulets in an Egyptian tomb. "Mademoiselle Chanel was born a Leo," said the guide, anticipating a question I had not yet asked. "The lion is the king of the animals, and her attitude was a royal one."

She motioned to me to stand up, so that we could examine the hidden doors, seamless in the paneled walls. "Mademoiselle did not like to see doors," said the guide, "because doors meant that people were leaving her. She wanted her own world around her, at all times."

And Chanel still makes her presence felt in this place, despite the force of its current ruler, Karl Lagerfeld (or, as he is more often known, though not to his face, "The Kaiser"). Her name remains on the door to the design studio where Lagerfeld prepares the collections, her portrait on the wall behind his desk; not that he appears anything other than entirely confident in his ability to confront that most challenging of ghosts. "I took her code, her language, and mixed it all up," he remarked, last time I interviewed him, in May 2004 for the Saturday *Telegraph* magazine, when he was surrounded by his murmuring retinue in the studio, on the eve of their latest catwalk show. "She had one idea, and didn't divert from it. But my job is to reinvent Chanel—so I have to play with the codes, kill them, even, before I use them again." As he spoke his eyes flicked over the models being presented to him, one by one, adjusting the details of the outfits for the next day's show; the camellia corsages on reinvented little black dresses and tweed suits. And though I knew that this was a man at the height of his power and influence (evidence of which was to be had not only in Chanel's rising profits, but also in chain stores, where copycat Lagerfeld was everywhere, and in the press, too, where the talk was all of his preeminence, and his famous diet, in which he had lost ninety pounds, and gained a new slimline wardrobe), I came away wondering if there were other ghosts around him, as well; and about the part the past might play in the inventions and predictions that are the stuff of fashion futures. His father, a Swedish industrialist who had made a fortune out of condensed milk, was sixty when Karl was born in Hamburg in 1938; his German mother forty-two. Karl was the only son; treated almost as an only child, he remarked to me, with a much older half-sister from his father's first marriage, and another older sister from the second. Both girls had been sent away to boarding school, and although Karl stayed at home, his parents were remote figures.

Interestingly—though I'm sure Lagerfeld would be quick to deny this—you get the sense that his parents might be closer at hand these days. He told me that his best design ideas appeared in dreams—"I have very clear visions of what I want to do, what I should do, what I could do"—but also "I have nightmares too, that I prefer not to talk about." Lagerfeld is clearly a man with no time for analysis—his is a career based on now, not then; on conscious desires, not subconscious fears—but what could be made of his admission that in his dreams, he hears only the voices of the dead, "never those who are alive"? His hands fluttered slightly as he talked, as if he were brushing something away; though his voice was gentle, as ever. "I just had a dream which was very funny," he continued. "My father died over thirty years ago, but I dreamt I was in his boardroom with him, and a lot of people who I didn't really know, I didn't know their faces, because I never worked with my father. And then they served lunch, and my father said to me, "You can't have lunch because you don't know how to use the Power-Book. You won't eat until you learn how to use it." My father died long before the PowerBook was invented, of course, but it was him, it was his voice, the way he dressed, the paneling in the boardroom, everything was there, exactly as I had seen as a child."

When I asked him what the link between eating and power could mean, he said, simply, "I don't know, it's strange." And of course, the dream resisted interpretation; though here is a man whose power within the industry has risen in a period when he has also eaten less; whose influence has grown larger as he has shrunk, as is often the case in the fashion business, where there is no such thing as being too thin. Yet even though he has reduced and reshaped his body, he must also be aware, always, of the fact that he is growing older, as his father did; that there may be no tomorrow, even though time, inexorably, moves on. ("Why does Karl always keep us waiting?" said a close friend of his, part of a court grown accustomed to their ruler's famous disregard for time-keeping. "He loves not having a clock, feeling free . . . time is entirely fluid, for him.")

As for those other ghosts in his life: well, there is his mother, who sounds sufficiently imperious in life to remain a powerful figure in death. ("She was the most formidable woman," remarked another friend, "beautiful, always exquisitely dressed, sometimes in Chanel, and extremely clever—clever enough to know how to wound. She's stayed very close to him, believe me.") Much of how Lagerfeld presents himself to the world today can still be attributed to his mother: he speaks fast, because she told him that otherwise she would not listen to him; he does not smoke, because she decreed that his hands were too ugly to draw attention to; he is multilingual, because there was no other way to follow her conversation. "I always wanted to be a grown-up person," he said to me, matter-of-factly, "because my mother said that children were stupid."

She sounds terrifying, I replied (thinking that she also seemed to have something in common with the famously cutting Mademoiselle Chanel).

"No, no, she was perfect for me," he said, "and she was always right. It was a good thing for me to try to speak like a grown-up person. She would tell me, 'You are six, but I am not, so make an effort.'"

And so he did make great efforts: "By five years old I could read English and Spanish. My father didn't like to speak

German, he spoke mostly English." (There is an often repeated story—possibly apocryphal—that at four he asked for his own valet; certainly, he requested a French tutor at that age.) As he talked to me about his childhood, he rapped the rings on his fingers on his desk; hard and quick, in time with his sentences, and I wondered whether that was something his mother did. Now he was thin, he said, he could fit into a Chanel tweed jacket—but he only tried this once, never again, because when he looked at himself in the mirror, he could see the reflection of his mother, which frightened him.

She is buried in the private chapel at the house he inherited from her in Brittany; so, too, is Jacques de Bascher, a wild French aristocrat and Lagerfeld's closest friend for nearly twenty years, who died of AIDS in 1989, at the age of thirty-seven. Lagerfeld has said in the past that the relationship was not sexual, though de Bascher's death precipitated a long period of mourning. Yet even before the pain of that loss, Lagerfeld had never veered from being, essentially, solitary; he did not share a house with de Bascher, nor has he done so with anyone subsequently. True, he has his retinue: an elegant coterie that includes Amanda Harlech, his muse and right-hand woman at Chanel, and Carine Roitfeld, editor of French *Vogue* (both of them supremely elegant models for his latest little black dresses). "But I nearly never go out," he said, "I am not glamorous at all, I stay in, because otherwise there is not enough time to do everything." And at the end of the day, as always, he goes to bed alone; a small single bed, the same one that he had as a child.

Unlike most other fashion designers I have met, Lagerfeld made no serious claims for himself, nor for the work he does. "I am very superficial," he said, gesturing toward a model in the latest Chanel tweed coat, "I think these are just clothes, no great theories behind it." He was equally pragmatic about his own appearance: "You know, I put on weight, because for ten years fashion was boring, and then suddenly something appeared that I wanted to wear."

The truth, perhaps, is a bit more complicated: because like all the best magicians, part of Lagerfeld's act is to make his conjuring tricks seem effortless; so easy that they appear natural, instead of hard-won. ("Karl once said to me that before he lost weight, he felt embalmed in fat," remarked Amanda Harlech; but Houdini-like, he escaped out of his fat-suit, walked away from the tomb.) "I think I don't need a wall any more between myself and the world," said Lagerfeld. "I think I got over the wall myself. It's like you're talking about another person—I don't remember him."

He also divested himself of other evidence of the past, selling much of his famous art collection, including rococo works by Fragonard and Boucher, and eighteenth-century furniture. "At the moment I want nothing," he said, "I like houses with space and light." He told me about his favorite one, a new house, which he was planning to remake: a castle in Champagne, the Château de l'Isle. There, he said, he wants a garden just like that in *The Others*, which is one of his favorite films; a ghost story that appears to be set in 1945, at the end of the Second World War, but where time has turned in on itself: where the dead are haunted by the living, as well as the other way round; where a mother has done something terrible to her children, in the name of love; where a house is surrounded by a misty garden that seems a kind of limbo; where the rest of the world—and its war—is kept at bay. (It is also a film that takes its title from a line in "The Turn of the Screw," and its ghosts are similarly well dressed; Nicole Kidman, in particular, wearing elegantly close-fitting suits that would not have looked out of place on Coco Chanel or her favorite models, which may have something to do with Kidman's subsequent casting in a Chanel No. 5 advertising campaign.)

When I saw Lagerfeld the following evening, I wanted to ask him more about his island castle and who his others were; but I couldn't get close enough to talk. The collection had been shown on a cruise boat; strict blazers with clouds of tulle and chiffon; softness played against toughness; silvery sequins against rough tweed; and little black dresses on the models and in the audience, too, as we all went sailing down the Seine. Afterward, I'd sat in a corner with Amanda Harlech (exquisitely correct in her clothes, but with a talent for conversational warmth, as well). She'd told me that Lagerfeld saw ghosts all around him, but he was always unperturbed; we talked about little black dresses, and how they were the negative of a wedding gown—traditionally worn by widows or divorcées—which was how they retained their power to subvert convention, when you saw them on a young girl. By then, the voyage had returned to the place it started from, and the Chanel models were stepping back on dry land again, amid an audience chirruping about the triumph of the show (the models still looking like another species, even though they had changed into jeans and T-shirts; all of them impossibly thin, none of them eating the food provided for them—except one, the youngest, who boldly ate a piece of pineapple from a platter of fruit). Lagerfeld remained on board, separated from us by the river water, standing on the top deck, still wearing his dark glasses, of course, so I couldn't tell what he was looking at; and there were a multitude of white balloons floating above him, bigger than the moon, and his head was tilted upward, at an unseen something in the darkening blue sky; or maybe there was nothing, maybe he could see nothing there at all.

11

The Women in White

"How shall I describe what we saw? On the bed lay two women, Lucy and her mother. The latter lay farthest in, and she was covered with a white sheet, the edge of which had been blown back by the draught through the broken window, showing the drawn, white face, with a look of terror fixed upon it. By her side lay Lucy, with face white and still more drawn. The flowers which had been round her neck we found upon her mother's bosom, and her throat was bare, showing the two little wounds which we had noticed before, but looking horribly white and mangled."

Bram Stoker, *Dracula*

"The snowflake grew bigger and bigger until it became at last a whole woman, dressed in the sheerest white gossamer, which looked as if it were made of millions of starlike flakes. She was so beautiful and elegant but made of ice, dazzling, glittering ice, and yet she was alive. Her eyes stared like two bright stars, but there was nothing calm or peaceful about them."

Hans Christian Andersen, *The Snow Queen*
translated by Tiina Nunnally

". . . and they shall walk with me in white, for they are worthy."

Revelation: 3, verse 4

I

WHEN I WAS A CHILD, still living in Oxford, I dreamed one night of my mother; except she wasn't my day-time mother, with her flaming red hair, but a moon-lit woman, porcelain-white. She didn't look like my mother, she wasn't my mother, but in the dream, I knew her to be mine. I was standing at the bottom of a long flight of stairs, and she was at the top—higher, even, than the highest landing in our tall Victorian house; for this was a different house from ours, grander, with long uncurtained windows overlooking a dark night-time garden, though like the alabaster figure above me, I recognized the landscape as well.

I looked at my dream-mother, and she was dressed all in white—a long shroud-like robe, less substantial than the Victorian white cotton nightdresses that my real mother wore—and then she stepped forward, and I cried out, but no sound came from my throat, I could not stop her as she fell to the bottom of the stairs. And when I went to touch her, she was shattered into pieces, like china, and there was nothing inside, no flesh, no blood, no body; but I knew that something terrible had happened, that my mother was dead and gone. Did she jump or was she pushed? I wasn't certain, though the nightmare recurred, night after night, and I could never save her; the arc of her swan dive was broken, over and over again.

The memory of that woman in white—the knowledge that she would fall, the sinister apprehension that she *wanted* to fall, and then the sight of her, smashed and fractured, still makes me shudder; and has doubtless infected my reading of other women in white, like Emily Dickinson, whom I came to after the White Witch in Narnia and Hans Christian Andersen's Snow Queen (though it might have been those women in white who provided the material for my nightmare). It was my mother who gave me a book of Emily Dickinson's poetry when I was nine or ten, round about the same time that I was having the nightmares; not that the two were necessarily connected, but when I remember them—the book and the dream—they seem to reflect each other. Oddly, although I now struggle with Dickinson's poetry—find her meaning increasingly elusive as I get older—as a child, the effort was less. The anthology my mother gave me was for children (its title was *I'm Nobody! Who Are You?*); it also contained biographical details, including a brief account of Dickinson's life within her father's house in Amherst, Massachusetts: a woman who wore only white dresses, who remained unseen, behind closed doors or in the shadows. I'd been told that one of her white dresses remains in her father's house, now a museum; though it seemed to me by the time I was a teenager that Dickinson had turned her room into a kind of museum when she was still alive, shutting herself away in it to write her poetry; not that she had planned to make an exhibition of herself, but nevertheless, I wondered whether she realized that interest in her would intensify after her decision to withdraw from view.

When my mother gave me the anthology, however, I was too young to think about what prompted Dickinson to become a white-clad recluse. (And I hadn't yet read Ted Hughes's description of her, in the introduction to his selection of her poetry: "she wore white, proper for a bride of the spirit, and she daily composed poems that read like devotions"). I was more interested in the poem that gave the title to my book, and also the one that began, "I started Early—Took my Dog— / And visited the Sea— / The Mermaids in the Basement / Came out to look at me—." I imagined Emily in her white dress, creeping out of her father's house at dawn, her dog by her side, when no one else could see her; and walking to the seaside, to find the mermaids, with their long pale hair, and beckoning hands. And the water was lapping around her feet, and higher ("—till the Tide / Went past my simple Shoe— / And past my Apron—and my Belt / And past my Bodice—too—"); so that she was up to her neck, her hair floating in the water like the mermaids'.

I don't remember reading her more opaque poetry at the time; it was only later that it got under my skin (her impenetrability, I mean, finding its way into me, yet remaining intact). But whenever I read it now, there are still lines that I recognize as if from childhood; for I have never studied Dickinson in a formal sense; never been educated in her meaning, always avoided critical dissection of her work (which may mean, of course, that my response to her is simply childish; though I am also inclined to agree with Thomas Wentworth Higginson, who wrote in the *Atlantic Monthly*, twenty years after meeting Dickinson, that her enshrouding was too complete to undo: "She was much too enigmatical a being for me to solve in an hour's interview . . . I could only sit still and watch, as one does in the woods; I must name my bird without a gun, as recommended by Emerson"). Sometimes I feel irritated with myself, with my failure to make sense of her work; but sometimes I like the fact that it remains out of reach, not analyzed, not unfolded. And when I don't understand the poems, there are things—clothes, named and made manifest—within them that can be recognized with the clarity of an often-repeated dream. So that now, when I read the poem that begins: "Because I could not stop for Death— / He kindly stopped for me" (lines that I remember as well as a nursery rhyme), I cannot help but see the translucent figure that emerges between the lines: "For only Gossamer, my Gown— / My Tippet—only Tulle—"

Not that I'm any closer to making sense of this woman in white; not even when Dickinson is at her most tantalizingly explicit. ("A solemn thing—it was—I said— / A woman— white—to be— / And wear—if God should count me fit— / Her blameless mystery.") Is she talking about a shroud or a wedding dress; a dress for first communion or a madwoman's hospital gown; angelic raiment or nun's habit or robes for the Bride of Christ who appears in another poem? ("Bride of the Father and the Son / Bride of the Holy Ghost.")

Despite her elusiveness, it was Emily Dickinson who led me to other women in white: to Emily Brontë (whom Dickinson admired) and her description of Cathy in *Wuthering Heights*, half-mad and sick after her marriage to Linton. ("Mrs. Linton sat in a loose, white dress, with a light shawl over her shoulders, in the recess of the open window, as usual.") And to Charlotte Brontë, of course, and Jane Eyre, who refuses Mr. Rochester's attempts to buy her an expensive silk trousseau, but even so, feels strangely dissociated from her bridal outfit on the evening before her (first, doomed) marriage ceremony: "for not to me appertained that suit of wedding raiment; the pearl-coloured robe, the vapoury veil . . . I shut the closet, to conceal the strange, wraith-like apparel it contained; which, at this evening hour—nine o'clock—gave out certainly a most ghostly shimmer through the shadow of my apartment. 'I will leave you by yourself, white dream,' I said." But the wraith-like clothes have already drawn to them—and Jane Eyre—another ghostly woman in white, the first Mrs.

Rochester, the madwoman descended from the attic. "It seemed, sir, a woman, tall and large, with thick and dark hair hanging long down her back," Jane tells Rochester. "I know not what dress she had on: it was white and straight; but whether gown, sheet, or shroud, I cannot tell." Jane says that the specter reminds her of "the foul German specter—the Vampyre"; and this Gothic vampire-bride dresses herself in Jane's wedding veil—"she held it up, gazed at it long, and then she threw it over her own head, and turned to the mirror"— before tearing it in two, "and flinging both on the floor, trampled on them."

The Brontëan women in white must also include the sisters themselves—at least, the fictionalized versions of them that appear in Mrs. Gaskell's *Life of Charlotte Brontë*, and other, subsequent biographies—whose virginal white was replaced by the shrouds of their early graves. I was of the generation of children that did not simply read the Brontë novels, but heard Kate Bush on the radio warbling her hit single about Heathcliff and Cathy; saw the books dramatized on the television (the terrifying ghost-child of *Wuthering Heights*, with her bleeding hand coming through the window; and crazy Mrs. Rochester, looming over a sleeping Jane Eyre); and the writers seemed to be characters come to life in that same, vividly *real*, yet Gothic world. Thus the Brontë tragedy was as well known to me as the plots of their novels: Anne died, unmarried, at twenty-nine, just a few months after her sister Emily, who was thirty, and their brother, Branwell, at thirty-one; their mother had also died in her thirties, leaving six small children, of whom the two oldest girls—Maria and Elizabeth—were dead within six weeks of each other, at the age of eleven and ten respectively. Charlotte, the last surviving child, who had mourned her mother and all five of her siblings, was the only one to be married, but her white wedding dress was followed, nine months later, by another Brontë shroud.

It was, perhaps, inevitable that I would progress from the Brontës and Emily Dickinson to an equally mythic Sylvia Plath, who describes herself in "Tulips" in hospital, on her sickbed; a patient, seeking the patience of a nun, colorless, day-clothes gone. ("Look how white everything is . . .") "I am nobody," says Plath in the same poem, echoing Emily Dickinson; and speaks of learning peacefulness. But as I kept on reading more of her poetry (as one does, in gloomy adolescence), she didn't seem very peaceful to me, unless you accepted that death bestowed peace (not that she *did* rest in peace); and the whiteness in her poems was as likely to signify bleached bones and death.

In fact, the more I looked (or rather, read), the more it seemed that women in white were inverted angels, mad, bad and dangerous to know; from the suicidal Anne Sexton, whose reworking of Snow White I had discovered among my mother's books of poetry, alongside Sylvia Plath, all the way back to Miss Havisham, who looms over *Great Expectations* like a risen corpse. (At first, when Pip makes her out in the gloom of her darkened, shuttered room, he believes her to be an entirely white figure: dress, shoes, veil, even her hair. But as his eyes grow accustomed to the shadows, "I saw that everything within my view which ought to be white, had been white long ago, and had lost its luster, and was faded and yellow. I saw that the bride within the bridal dress had withered like the dress, and like the flowers, and had no brightness left but the brightness of her sunken eyes. I saw that the dress had been put upon the rounded figure of a young

119

woman, and that the figure upon which it now hung loose, had shrunk to skin and bone." Two decades after the publication of *Great Expectations*, Emily Dickinson was directly compared to Miss Havisham by Mabel Todd, the family friend who later undertook the editing of Dickinson's poetry; she noted in her journal of 1882 that "Emily is called in Amherst 'the myth.' She has not been out of the house for fifteen years. One inevitably thinks of Miss Haversham in speaking of her . . . She wears always white, & has her hair arranged as was the fashion fifteen years ago, when she went into retirement.")

To be honest, by the time I was sixteen or so, they were all beginning to get me down a bit, these women in white—the very opposite of hopeful innocents—particularly as my sister (who was undergoing an even gloomier adolescent episode than me) had found a recording of Sylvia Plath's poetry, and had taken to playing it at full volume in her bedroom, as if in angry opposition to my father, who was downstairs blasting out an equally loud record of Ted Hughes reading his charred-dark "Crow" poems. (The man in black versus the girl in white, with me irritated beyond all measure in the middle.) I had by then discovered—as a certain type of bookish teenage girl tends to do—that Sylvia Plath and Ted Hughes had gone to Haworth together, making poetry out of their walks through the graveyard beside the Brontë parsonage and up onto the moors of Wuthering Heights. And I knew, too, that Emily Dickinson was an admirer of Emily Brontë, whose poetry had been read at her funeral, and that Plath and Hughes were fans of both Emilys, and that you could draw threads between all four poets (and Dickens and Wilkie Collins, as well); white threads, probably . . .

But I wasn't sufficiently melancholic to want to undertake a full-blown immersion in their myths; possibly because I had already encountered that nightmarish woman in white of my own (a dream wraith that I was doing my best to forget). It's only recently, a quarter of a century later, that I've found myself intrigued by the subject of women in white again. Of course, now that *The Woman in White* is a long-running and profitable West End musical—its name more attached to Andrew Lloyd Webber than Wilkie Collins's original novel—it's easy to forget how powerfully unsettling this phrase must once have been. Collins had had some difficulty in coming up with the title for his novel, which was to be serialized in Dickens's magazine *All the Year Round*—despite having already written the opening chapter, including its eerie encounter on a moonlit road with a "solitary Woman, dressed from head to foot in white"—but when he did decide upon it, in August 1859, and sent it to Dickens for his approval, Dickens replied: 'I have not the slightest doubt that The Woman in White is the name of names, and very title of titles.'

In fact, Dickens had already described a woman in white of his own, some years earlier, in 1853, in an autobiographical essay entitled "Where We Stopped Growing" in his magazine *Household Words*. She was a figure from his London boyhood, he wrote, seen always on Berners Street: "whether she was constantly on parade in that street only, or was ever to be seen elsewhere, we are unable to say. The White Woman is her name. She is dressed entirely in white, with a ghastly white plaiting round her head and face, inside her white bonnet. She even carries (we hope) a white umbrella. With white boots, we know she picks her way through the winter dirt. She is a conceited old creature, cold and formal in manner, and evidently went simpering mad on personal grounds alone—no doubt because a wealthy Quaker wouldn't marry her. This is her bridal dress."

There is one more, small, pleasing (to me) connection to be made between all these women in white: which comes in a warning by the artist James Whistler *not* to make connections. His painting of his redheaded mistress in a white dress (*Symphony in White, No. 1: The White Girl*) was assumed by many when it was exhibited in 1862 to be an illustration of Collins's immensely popular novel; but in a letter to the *Athenaeum*, whose art critic had made the link, Whistler wrote: "May I beg to correct an erroneous impression likely to be confirmed by a paragraph in your last number? The Proprietors of the Berners Street Gallery have, without my sanction, called my picture 'The Woman in White.' I had no intention whatsoever of illustrating Mr. Wilkie Collins's novel; it so happens, indeed, that I have never read it. My painting simply represents a girl dressed in white standing in front of a white curtain." It is tempting to speculate about whether anyone from his art gallery remembered the same well-known woman in white that Dickens had described, parading up and down Berners Street. But Whistler's point is a better one: that a woman in white does not need to be viewed as part of a historical or social or moral or psychoanalytic narrative; her depiction can be nothing more than an exercise in light and tone.

Even so, most of us recognize a woman in white from our own pasts or imagination or dream-life; the thwarted or sinister bride of Dracula; the wedding dress turned shroud; doomed Princess Diana, the fairy-tale virgin bride on her way to an early grave; Snow White, poisoned and lifeless; the pale, veiled ghost or the Lady of Shalott or the snow queen with a frozen heart. All of which might seem like a long way away from the fashion catwalk, but it's not entirely, in an industry that is engaged in the subversion, as well as the celebration, of feminine archetypes. Of course, it's hard to pin down, precisely, what is signified by a designer's use of white; or why it suddenly takes hold of the imagination; but what is true is that white is always open to varying interpretation, given that it is the color of mourning in some Eastern cultures, and has been so in the West, as well. There is some speculation that Emily Dickinson started wearing white dresses after the death of her father; and when the Queen Mother went on a state visit to France in 1938, not long after the death of *her* mother, she took with her a specially commissioned white wardrobe designed by Norman Hartnell. She left Buckingham Palace dressed in black, and stepped from the Royal Train in Paris in white; which was appropriate, given that French queens had worn white mourning until the seventeenth century, and Mary, Queen of Scots wore "deuil blanc" as a young widow in France. Not that the Hartnell dresses were simply following an ancient precedent: in one of those oddly perverse inconsistencies that often mark the shifts of fashion, the widespread craze for black dresses in the Roaring Twenties was superseded, after "Black Friday" and the crash of 1929, by a new vogue for white that lasted throughout most of the thirties; a decade with a darker mood, despite its prevailing style, characterized by Coco Chanel as "candid innocence and white satin."

Yet despite Chanel's love of aphorism, I've never come across anything that suggests she analyzed what was responsible for her own shift from little black dresses—made to be lithe and lively—to more ethereal white creations. Colette, who described Chanel as "a small black bull . . . in her butting energy, in her way of facing up to things," wrote an intriguing portrait of her at work in 1932 (published in *Prisons et paradis*), that suggests the conflicting impulses between the earthy and unearthly: "Mademoiselle Chanel is engaged in sculpting an angel 6 feet tall. A golden-blond angel, impersonal, seraphically beautiful, providing one disregards the rudimentary carving, the paucity of flesh, and the cheerlessness—one of those angels who brought the devil to earth.

"The angel—still incomplete—totters occasionally under the two creative, severe, kneading arms that press against it. Chanel works with ten fingers, nails, the edge of the hand, the palms, with pins and scissors right on the garment, which is a white vapor with long pleats, splashed with crushed crystal. Sometimes she falls to her knees before her work and grasps it, not to worship but to punish it again, to tighten over the angel's long legs—to constrain—some expansion of tulle . . ."

It's a description that might still be applied to the making of the white wedding dresses that have traditionally provided a finale to the Paris couture shows; splendid bridal confections that provide substantial orders for some of the most prestigious fashion houses, yet which are also expected to reveal a new or unexpected design twist. For example, the closing sequence of John Galliano's couture show for Dior in January 2005 featured a series of ethereal white or ivory gowns—a reminder, perhaps, of the concurrent publicity coup that had seen Donald Trump's newest wife in Dior bridal couture on the front cover of American *Vogue*—but on the catwalk, the designer had added what looked like pregnant or malignant swellings beneath his floor-length, empire-line creations. At the end, Galliano appeared to take the final bow, looking devilish in piratical black.

A few days afterward, I was talking about all this to Erin O'Connor, who had modeled in the Dior show, and was passing through London on her way to New York fashion week. "To me, it looked like these girls had been abused in some way," she said, describing the procession of doll-faced pregnant-looking brides. "They were virgins who had been violated and tampered with, but still in those very expensive, luxurious white gowns." The white dresses were beautiful, she added, 'and they were also disturbing, but isn't that what you know to expect by now?' And she was right, though it's interesting how often contemporary fashion reporting ignores that twist between beauty and horror on the catwalk: perhaps because when you're close to those dresses, you can see only the rarefied art and exquisite work that has gone into their making; it is only from a distance that they look more sinister.

II

On a recent visit to Lesage—one of the five Parisian ateliers owned by Chanel, this specializing in the most intricate embroidery for all the leading design houses—I was shown into a room where half a dozen women were hand-sewing thousands of antique sequins and pearls onto a long white gown, a Chanel wedding dress for a couture client. "When a dress is made by a machine, the soul is gone," remarked François Lesage, whose family-run business has provided exquisite hand-work for Chanel, along with the other couturiers, for more than fifty years. "That's why we still work in the same way as in the nineteenth century." When I asked Monsieur Lesage who could afford such a dress, and how much it cost, he just smiled, and raised his palms toward the ceiling. "You know, in the crash of 1929, no one was buying anything—Lesage nearly closed—and there have been times since then when the climate is difficult. But there are always clients who don't even need to ask the price."

The wedding dress was most likely being made for the fiancée of a Russian billionaire or an Arab princess or an American heiress; but for some reason, the face that flashed into my head was that of a dead woman, who I hadn't thought of in several years: Wallis Franken, the former wife and muse of the fashion designer Claude Montana. It sounds morbid, I know, though truthfully, I was thinking not of her death, but of the pictures I'd seen of her Parisian wedding, when she'd been the most chic of brides; as you might expect from a famous catwalk model marrying an equally famous designer, in the middle of couture week. I'd never met her: she died in Paris in May 1996, three years after the wedding, swan-diving from the kitchen window of the Montana apartment in the rue de Lille. When her body was found in the courtyard, she was wearing black leggings and a torn white shirt; after the autopsy and a brief police investigation, the French authorities ruled her death to have been a suicide.

By the time I interviewed her husband, in October 1998 for the *Sunday Telegraph* magazine, the rumor and gossip about their ill-fated marriage had not yet abated in fashion circles. Claude Montana was gay, but it was more complicated than a 'mariage blanc,' because Wallis had loved and championed him ever since they'd first met, in the seventies, when she was among the most successful models in Paris, and he was starting out as a designer. Of course, the wedding in July 1993 seemed odd: she was a wide-smiled American with two daughters from a previous marriage; he had become almost as notorious for his nightclubbing as his dark dominatrix creations that had defined a hard-edged eighties aesthetic, alongside the glacial ice-maidens that stalked through Montana shows. But Wallis Franken was still his favorite model, and she was married to him in an outfit of his own creation: high-collared, with long ruffled cuffs; a trouser suit, though it had something very dressy about it, also; meticulously fitted, as always, and white, of course (Montana was as celebrated for his white tailoring as his black leather). The wedding was much discussed, for the fashion press was gathered in Paris for the couture shows: the bride and groom departed in a white stretch limo; he was wearing a buck-skin suede suit and snakeskin boots; she looked radiant in the wedding photographs that appeared in *Hello!*

My meeting with Claude Montana took place five years later, after what had been billed as his comeback show. Business had been very bad for him the previous year, though his name still carried weight—sufficient to pull in big new investment for this show, which in the skewed world of fashion was part of the spring/summer 1999 collections. So while it was a leaden and drizzling autumnal day outside, in the vaulted subterranean halls of the Carrousel du Louvre, hundreds of feet below the streets of Paris, we were gathered to watch girls in shorts and bikinis, backless dresses and strapless tops; or rather, that's what I saw at the other shows. At Montana, there was not much in the way of sunshiny clothes, but his characteristic slash of zippers, strict black dresses, all-in-one leather catsuits, rock-chick miniskirts. "Is that all there is?" crooned the song on the soundtrack for the show. "If that's all there is, then let's keep dancing. Let's break out the booze and have a ball, if that's all there is . . . If that's all."

At the end, there was polite applause, and the audience filed out, on to the next shows, to Sonia Rykiel and John Galliano. But I was among the small group with appointments to go backstage: Japanese film crews, mainly, and a few alarming-looking women with severe bobs and leather trousers. The new president of the house of Montana was hovering—a plump man, perspiring in his double-breasted suit (because it was as hot as hell down there). "We have lots of plans," he said, peering distractedly over my shoulder toward a small tent in the far corner of the backstage area. "Montana has a strong market in France and Germany, and there is great potential in England. Business collapsed a year ago, but it's a resuming fast. People are ready to start again."

I realized, after being ushered to a queue outside the tent, that Montana was hidden within it, like a circus sideshow. In front of us stood an elderly Japanese woman in black platform boots and a Chanel suit; it was her turn next, and then mine, if I could make it past the entrance to the tent, guarded by Claude's sister, Jacqueline, who was in charge of his PR. She was wearing an all-black Montana uniform: immaculate polo neck with padded shoulders, precisely cut trousers, sharp stiletto boots; but in her hand she held a pale rose, wilting in the heat, petals turning papery-white like the tissues scattered on the floor beneath our feet, discarded by the make-up artists before the show.

Eventually, Jacqueline Montana beckoned to me to go into the tent, but it took a few seconds to adjust to the stale twilight inside, to focus on the uncertain-looking little man sitting there, in tight jeans, red satin bomber jacket, hooded top and cowboy boots; his mustache as carefully combed as his coiffed hair. Beads of sweat broke out on his nose and forehead through the thick white makeup. He looked vulnerable, fragile, and yet also extraordinary, like the Wizard of Oz unveiled from behind a curtain.

By now, the stagehands were dismantling the set, and he winced at the loud bangs outside the tent. "I hate that noise," he lisped, very quietly, between sips of champagne. "It's so upsetting."

I had already been warned by his sister that I was forbidden to ask any questions about Wallis, and about the circumstances of her suicide. Instead, we were to talk about his new collection, though it seemed bizarre, discussing clothes while skirting around Wallis, the muse who must not be mentioned.

"I decided to work with the colors I feel most comfortable with," whispered Montana, when I commented on the preponderance of white and black in this collection (as was usual in his monochromatic shows). "I always follow my intuition. I try to be faithful to myself. There are different currents in fashion. If you try too much, too hard, to follow them, then you're totally lost. In this kind of work, sometimes you are at the top, sometimes you go down, and sometimes back up again. You cannot stay in a straight line. You also need to make mistakes."

I asked him if he had made any mistakes, and his sister—who had joined us inside the tent for the interview, Claude's first since Wallis's death—stiffened slightly, and seemed to hold her breath. He looked surprised, hurt, but answered me, nevertheless. "When I did the first Lanvin collection," he said, referring to his debut couture show for the house of Lanvin in

1989, now admired by many as modernist, but dismissed by others at the time, "it wasn't a mistake, but people didn't understand. I was totally destroyed by the press, and destroyed inside. If it had been someone else, the press wouldn't have gone so far. Perfection doesn't exist, but I tried very hard."

In my notebook, I wrote PERFECTION in capital letters, and then, "What is fashion but the search for perfection? To capture it somehow—the perfect cut of a white shirt—is this what drew Claude and Wallis together?" And I suppose, in looking for an answer to that inelegantly phrased question, I was also trying to capture Wallis on the page; though it seemed hard for those who survived her to agree on the right words to describe her to me. "She was dead-eyed, like anyone snorting a lot of coke," said a friend of mine who had been at the Montana wedding party; but then I spoke to Wallis's younger daughter, Celia, shortly after I'd interviewed Claude. "She was so amazing, so perfect," said Celia about her mother. "She was beautiful, strong, incredible. She was never unhappy, always ready to have fun."

"So why did she kill herself?" I asked.

"I don't know," said Celia. "To me, her daughter, she didn't look like a woman who wanted to die. But you never know. I'd like to think that suicide was a way out for her."

Celia was twenty when her mother married Claude, and like Wallis, had worked for him. So she'd been around the two of them often enough to know that "there was an attraction, even though he was gay. They loved each other." But things had soured; she had witnessed terrible arguments between the two of them. "People go crazy and . . . *voilà*. I don't hate him. It won't help me to hate him. It just happened."

I asked Celia if she still saw Claude. "No," she replied, "he threw me out straight after she died, and I didn't want to work there anymore, anyway. Now I'm a poker dealer in a casino. I'm a bit like Wallis—there's a lot of misery, but I'm still here. The Frankens, we keep going . . ."

What stopped Wallis Franken from keeping going? And what keeps Claude Montana going, still? The glib answer would be "fashion"; for it was fashion that made Wallis famous as a teenage model; and it was fashion that made her redundant at forty-eight, and so she killed herself. But for her husband, the designer, it was different: as he said to me, in his backstage tent, he still loved fashion, and he always would. "It's constantly exciting—a burden, sometimes, but in the end, always exciting. When you see the people around you, working hard for you, it touches me so deeply."

It wasn't a sufficient answer, however; just as it wasn't a good enough explanation for their marriage. What was Claude thinking of when he designed Wallis's virginal white wedding outfit? What were they thinking of that day when they made their vows? Certainly, they both believed in the importance of keeping up appearances: Wallis was raised in Westchester County, New York; her mother, Dorothy, had been a model; her father, Randolph, was the son of Leo Franken, a German who founded a string of women's fashion stores in America at the turn of the twentieth century. Randolph's first wife was a Ziegfeld showgirl; after a short-lived marriage, he married Dorothy in 1939. They had three children, but his family fortune was dwindling; by the time Wallis was in high school, the Frankens had moved to a smaller house, in a town called Pleasantville, and Randolph had taken a job as a salesman in a men's store on Fifth Avenue. When Randolph became ill, there were more financial anxieties that they kept to themselves; but Wallis was quick to start earning her own living, so that in 1967, the year her father died, she was already a very successful model. And the following year, when she was still only twenty, she fell in love with the man who was to become her first husband, Philippe de Henning, a handsome racing-car driver. They had two daughters, Rhea and Celia; their third child, a boy, died in a crib death when he was three months old. The marriage never really recovered after the baby's death, but Wallis and Philippe remained friends. When I talked to Philippe (who had by then converted to Scientology), he offered no clues about what had prompted her suicide. He knew that she had been taking drugs—the autopsy revealed that her body contained cocaine, as well as alcohol—but nothing seemed too awry. "She didn't have a problem with drugs," he said. "She had an astounding capacity for them. But she knew her limits." Nor did she give any indication of there being other problems in her life. "When I saw her ten days or so before she died, she seemed fine. She wanted to see the girls. She had plans . . ." For a moment, he sounded less calm. "It's paradoxical. It's astonishing that she should do such a thing. She had never talked about suicide, never." But the moment passed. "Wallis would never have wanted any controversy. She wasn't interested in accusations. It was just a passionate story that ended the way it ended. You can't hold anyone responsible."

I got no further with Montana, as you might expect. He'd told me very little about his parents—the son of a German mother and a Spanish father, he was born in Paris in 1949, when his father was serving in the French navy—but had expressed more enthusiasm on the subject of his aunt, or, to be more precise, her clothes. "I thought my mother's sister was terribly elegant," he said. "She used to wear gray flannel suits made by a man's tailor, with black lingerie underneath the jacket. I remember her arriving to visit in a brown mink coat, crocodile shoes, and a lavender chiffon skirt. She looked so beautiful."

Seeing his face light up for the first time, as he described his aunt's outfit, you could see why clothes mattered so much to him; and why, perhaps, he had loved Wallis, the woman who modeled his designs with such elegance. So I took the plunge and asked him the unmentionable question: would he tell me about his wife? He looked stunned, but I plowed on: we have to talk about Wallis, I said; you can't expect me to write about the Montana look without referring to her, with her sleek dark suits and white shirts and bobbed hair, elegantly androgynous. "She did not look like that when I met her," said Claude, finally, peevishly. "She was very American, a hippy with long frizzy hair. I became like a Pygmalion to her. Then she started to become more sophisticated. But for me, there were few facets to her. She was not iconic."

I asked him if he missed her. "I miss her a lot," he said. "Not only the way she dressed, but her sensibility. But unfortunately, she was not able to use what she had inside. She was so insecure about herself. She could have been a singer, she could have done plenty of things. I think the main problem was that she started modeling at sixteen, and she became famous immediately. She was treated like a star. Then she stopped modeling after a very long career, and she had nothing. She was used to people taking care of her."

His voice trailed away, but I kept going (like in a dream, when you say the things that you know should not be said). I asked him if he liked women, if the severity of his designs revealed an ambivalence in his feelings about them, perhaps a kind of contempt. He looked even more taken aback than before, when I had raised the subject of his dead wife. "I respect women," he said, sounding genuinely shocked. "I love women. I don't want women to look ridiculous. I make flattering clothes for women to wear."

Inevitably, the interview was brought to a close by my breach of etiquette; Montana's sister looked at her watch, and looked at me, but I didn't follow her gestured lead toward the tent door. What, I asked, trying not to sound desperate, were his plans for the future? "My future is in the hand of God," he said, which was not an answer I had expected.

"You believe in God?" I said.

"I believe in God. He will decide what my future will be."

Did he go to church as a child? "Always," he answered. "My mother was Protestant, my father was Catholic. I went to Sunday school. It was very strict."

It must have been hard, I said, for him to have reconciled being gay with that kind of upbringing. Montana shrank back away from me, further into his seat. His sister shook her head at me, as did another PR woman, who had arrived in the tent (as if bringing in reinforcements). You must not say such things, the women said. Monsieur Montana is a devout Protestant. They stepped toward me, ready to pull me out, if necessary, but Montana cleared his throat. He had one more thing to tell me. "I was taught that if you behave well, nothing bad will ever happen to you," he said. "I found out later that this was not true."

More than six years have now passed since that interview, and my path has never crossed Montana's again. He lives a secluded life, but his business has survived, with new investment; his name has been used to launch new perfumes, with some success, and he has designed a menswear collection, as well as his women's lines.

As for Wallis Franken: I'm no closer to knowing what passed through her mind in the moments before her final swan dive. And there isn't a definitive conclusion, of course; other than her ending, in her torn white shirt, on the ground beneath an open window. But I think her friend Maxine de la Falaise put it best, when she was interviewed by Maureen Orth in *Vanity Fair*. Claude Montana, she said, was like Wallis's "dark angel." But finally, "she did what I think of as flying away . . . I believe that she took off as a free spirit out of the window. She found life too oppressive, and she flew away like a bird."

To Die For . . .

Two short stories, as told to me by Erin O'Connor.

First, her memory of appearing on the catwalk in London for Alexander McQueen's spring/summer 2001 collection: a show that was much admired for its creative depiction of a "fashion asylum"; or, in Erin's words, "the lunatic show," in which the models had white bandaged heads. In it, she wore a white dress made out of razor shells—all of them collected by McQueen himself, from a Norfolk beach—that had taken weeks, if not months, to make. "And he told me just before I stepped out that he wanted me to go really mad—that he wanted me to rip off the dress onstage. And I said, 'Are you sure?' Because it's a beautiful dress, and he kind of gets carried away, and it's all pandemonium—and he shouts, 'Yeah! Just do it!' So off I go, I rip the dress, but the razor shells rip up my hands, as well. Afterward, I go backstage, for sympathy, saying, 'Look, my hands are really bleeding. Has anyone got any antiseptic wipes?' And the hair and makeup people say, 'Oh, *MAJOR!* Wipe your hands all over your bandage, it'll look great, because your next dress is blood-red.' So that's what I ended up doing—no one had any antiseptic, and I didn't have anywhere else to put my bleeding hands . . ."

Thus she realized, not for the first time in her career, that if beauty was in the eye of the beholder, then there were some in the fashion industry who saw beauty in "suffering, tragedy, literally being strung up . . ." A second lesson in the art of suffering for her beauty came at a more recent Paris catwalk show: "We all learned, very quickly, that you can't put on a thirteen-inch corset and wear thirteen-inch platform stilettos, with an enormous hooped skirt . . . And I had the biggest dress, right at the end of the show—the finale piece—and I couldn't handle it, I just wasn't tough enough, physically."

Erin didn't faint, she explained: "though I'd fainted the season before, when I came off the stage. But this time, I was feeling very ill. And actually, I couldn't faint and fall on the floor, because of my outfit—it was like wearing a balloon, and I had a metal waistband that was about half an inch thick, around me, supporting the hoops . . . Can you imagine, a thirteen-inch waist, and you're bearing the weight of another corset on top, in platform shoes so high that you can't feel your feet when you step? Every time I took a step, I was falling forward . . . I couldn't have *imagined* the horror of it all, it was like a nightmare."

While she was still backstage, waiting to go on, other models were falling on the catwalk; but in the end, the firemen who were on duty backstage prevented her from making her entrance. "They said, 'Non, finis.' They pointed out that my arms and legs had gone blue . . . And the next day, when I got up, I had lots of bruises on my legs—not from where I'd been hitting into things, but little blood veins had popped, all over."

"How very sinister," I said.

"That's right," she replied. "But you know what? It's my job."

12

Bella Donna

I'VE NEVER BEEN the obvious type to wear Versace—I'm not a Hollywood star or a trophy wife and though I do own two Versace pieces, I like them precisely because they're near-impossible to attribute to any label. (One is a pair of jeans: faded, narrow, beautifully cut, and flattering, in a way that suggests a woman had a part in their design; the other a short-sleeved cream sweater which has always looked desirably worn, as do the jeans, neither of them flaunting their newness; more evidence, now that I come to think of it, of clever design; and not at all the kind of extravagant display that is usually associated with Versace.)

But even though I'm not a regular Versace customer, I'm intrigued by Donatella Versace, who is most often presented as the living embodiment of the label; its mannequin made flesh. On the rare occasions that I've found myself in her vicinity, she emanates the most extraordinarily visceral power, making herself impossible to ignore. I'd seen her work the room at the 2002 *Vanity Fair* Oscar party in Los Angeles, seen her in her star-printed dress on the red carpet outside, posing for hundreds of photographers as they screamed out her name, her high-wattage hair more than a match for their camera flashes;

a hard-core exotic beside whom even Hollywood princesses were dimmed. And I saw her, too, in the summer of 1999, when she hosted a party at Syon House in London in aid of several cancer charities: an event for which she shipped in a diamond-shaped glass catwalk and several tons of Swarovski crystals, and then presided over the high table beside Prince Charles, Elizabeth Hurley and Hugh Grant; queen of the night in dazzling jewels, the absolute incarnation of that era's synthesis of money and fashion and celebrity; riding the crest of the wave of power and success. But none of this had prepared me for Donatella close up, when I interviewed her for the Saturday *Telegraph* magazine, toward the end of 2003.

It was eight months before she had checked into a drug-rehabilitation clinic to be treated for her addiction to cocaine, and though her problem was an open secret in the fashion industry, it was clearly not a subject that was open for discussion during the interview. In fact, while I waited for her to arrive at the Versace headquarters in Milan, I wasn't entirely sure that the interview would even take place, given that previous appointments had been postponed. And it was hard not to feel despondent when I was taken on a brief tour of the building, a palazzo on Via Gesu, as if in diversion from my main purpose. It was a raw wintry day, and everything looked a little desolate in the cold gray light: outside, in the gardens beyond the main building, was a tent still standing from previous fashion shows, its canvas roof half-covered in dying leaves; inside, the back staircase that led to the famous atelier looked slightly unkempt, with a couple of rough patches of plasterwork on the walls, and overflowing ashtrays on the landings. There was no obvious sign of the trademark Versace opulence, except in the clothes that were being worked upon in the attic floors: beautiful translucent pieces of jewel-colored chiffon and silk; pinned like butterflies by the white-coated women in the atelier.

I was surprised, too, by the odd air of impermanence, as well as history in the Versace palazzo: aside from the tent, there was another temporary structure in the central courtyard of this former monastery—iron girders and scaffolding that could be covered over with canvas for parties or presentations; incongruous against the old stone walls. But maybe that was as it should be, in a place dedicated to fashion, to the endless cycle of change and reinvention; yet a temple of reverence also, to Versace past, as well as present. It was here that Donatella's older brother, Gianni Versace, had his private apartment— where he lived, as well as worked, before his murder in 1997— and his legacy hangs over the building. For this is the house that Gianni built; this is his last testament; and his face still stares down from the walls—a huge photograph, diagonally sliced in two, cut in half with perfect precision, somber eyes following anyone who walks inside.

It was there, beneath Gianni's portrait, that I happened to be standing when Donatella finally arrived (though this may have been prearranged, given that Versace is a business that knows the importance of precise positioning). The door beside me swung open, letting in a gust of cold air from the courtyard outside, and the cavalcade made an entrance—Gianni's little sister, all grown up now, surrounded by bodyguards and assistants and her personal makeup artist and hairdresser. She was dressed entirely in black, I had time to see that— black spiky boots, sharp black trousers, black cashmere top—but she did not pause, walked straight into the room where she was to be interviewed and photographed; gone in a flurry of walkie-talkies and rushed importance, though the door wouldn't stop creaking; "Like a ghost," said one of the Versace press officers, wincing at the noise.

What, I wondered, would Gianni Versace have made of this Donatella—his Donatella—now? The girl whose dark hair he dyed blonde when she was eleven—a decade younger than him—once upon a time in faraway southern Italy, where they grew up in Reggio di Calabria; the sister who followed him north to Milan, when he launched his fashion business in 1978; the rising star they called his muse, whose influence within the company grew when Gianni was being treated for cancer in 1996; the woman who kept right on working, keeping the show on schedule, after her brother was shot dead by a gunman outside his mansion in Miami Beach. The Versace symbol might be the famous Medusa head that gazes out, implacable, from every label and price tag; but Donatella is the real face of Versace; and she can do the basilisk stare as well as anyone can.

She was doing it for the photographer when I was allowed into the room: not a hint of a smile, eyes unblinking at the camera; perfect lips pouting, as if ready to snarl. "This is Donatella dressed down," murmured another press officer— she had changed out of her black working uniform for the photographs, into jeans and pink sandals and a fabulously pretty print blouse from the new spring collection—but she looked ferocious even so; altogether as astonishing a creation as her mane of platinum hair extensions; as hard and as bright and as beautiful as the big diamonds she wore on her hands. Between each shot for the camera, a flunky poured her a fresh glass of iced water, which she sipped through a straw; and the hairdresser hovered, to fluff everything up. She looked scary, I thought, like someone you wouldn't want to cross; but there was something breakable about her, as well, like a cross between Rapunzel and a voodoo doll; a character from a fairy tale as told by the Brothers Grimm.

That curious mix of fragility and implacable hardness was even more apparent during my interview with her—not that it was an interview in much more than name, for she seemed in no mood for conversation. The odd thing about all of this—the stoniness, the silence—was that it wasn't what I was expecting. Quite aside from my absurdly misguided idea that I would be able to find the right words to ask her about her brother's death—that she would want to talk to me, because I had lost a sibling, too; that we might have something to share—I had been told that she was far more approachable than her appearance suggested. And it wasn't only her friends who had emphasized that she was sweet, lovable, good-hearted and generous-spirited—I'd heard that, also, from former employees, who had no apparent reason to spin the truth. ("She went out of her way to be welcoming not only to me, but to my boyfriend," said one of them, who had left Versace several years before. "She is inspiring to work for, and a wonderful mother to her children.") More compliments came flying in from elsewhere; and though that's how it tends to work when you interview a major player in the fashion world—there is a convention that the designer's friends and associates will provide endorsements—the people I talked to seemed genuinely affectionate about her, as opposed to simply finding her useful. Elizabeth Hurley, for example, said, "I like Donatella enormously; she's very funny and irreverent. She is also the only woman in the world I'd swap closets with." And Rupert

Everett, who has known Donatella for twenty years, spoke of her with real warmth. "She'll do anything for her friends," he said to me, when I was back in London. "She's completely loyal, as well as being honest and tender and brave."

Yet for all that, a kind of heaviness hung over my encounter with Donatella; dark like the draped curtains drawn against the light in the room where we sat. It was a ground-floor salon, thick with the scent of her favorite tuberose candles and bouquets of flowers, lined with mirrored doors, like a scene in *Alice Through the Looking-Glass* (and was it my imagination, or did Donatella have something of Alice about her; as if Alice had disappeared through a mirror and come out the other side, forty years older, almost to her surprise?).

She was back in her all-black clothes for the interview—the jeans and floral shirt were for the camera only—but it wasn't just her outfit that was somber, shut away and somehow closed. First of all, there was the impenetrability of her voice: viscous like treacle mixed with the tar of a billion cigarettes; difficult to understand, despite the fact that her English was fluent. And even after she removed her black shades, I couldn't read her eyes—couldn't tell if she was angry or sad or bored—and maybe she was all those things, or none of them, but she was obscured in the smoke of her endless cigarettes, blurred by what seemed to be a heavy cold, a handkerchief constantly covering her nose. "Or maybe it's the pollution?" observed Jason Weisenfeld, Versace's charming communications director, who sat beside the uncommunicative Donatella for the duration of the interview, prompting her when the silences become too uncomfortable. "The pollution is very bad in Milan today—it's not good for allergies."

I had already been warned by various members of the

Versace press team that I was not to ask Donatella about the financial details of the business. Indeed, I'd been briefed at considerable length to ignore the speculation that the unthinkable might happen, that someone outside the family—Tom Ford, perhaps—might take over at Versace. Yes, said the press team, it had been a challenging past year for Versace, just as it had for the rest of the luxury goods market—and how could it not be, after the impact of the war in Iraq?—but the situation was steadily improving, under the watchful eyes of Donatella's older brother, Santo Versace, who had successfully dealt with the business side of the company from the very start.

Instead, I had been advised to ask Donatella about her beauty routine (given that her personal choices were directly reflected in Versace's profitable and much admired range of makeup and skin products); and her outlook on life as a woman—as a working mother, and so on. "She's very shy," I'd been told by a Versace press person in one of many preparatory sessions before what was beginning to seem like a royal audience. "Why don't you talk about that?"

So that was where we started. "Yes, I am shy," said Donatella (though "said" is not nearly sufficient a verb to describe the way she sounded, like gravel in a glass of champagne). "Most of the time I'm bored at parties. I want to leave." And though the evidence in the room was that Donatella's friends equalled her in fame—a silver-framed photograph of Catherine Zeta-Jones clutching her Oscar in a black Versace dress, across which is written: "Dearest Donatella, A friend to cherish, I love you, Catherine," alongside a signed picture of Madonna and her children—she nevertheless insisted, "My real friends are not very famous. I don't go to parties for fun. I go to parties for work. In my real life, I like to spend time with a few friends at home, eating with them, watching videos, gossiping, talking. And I like to stay at home with my children—we talk about music and movies, we talk about everything. That's my idea of a perfect day—being with the kids and no phones, just shopping or watching football."

I found it hard to imagine Donatella doing those ordinary motherly things—she seemed like a widowed and solitary queen; even though I knew she had two teenage children with her ex-husband, Paul Beck: Daniel, who was then thirteen, and seventeen-year-old Allegra, both of whom lived with Donatella in Milan. (Beck was still working for Versace, as he had done for many years, commuting between Milan and his native New York. A former male model who had also been a good friend of Gianni's, he married Donatella in 1983, and they separated after Gianni's death.) I knew, too, that Allegra was due to inherit half of the company, as specified in Gianni's will, when she turned eighteen; and would therefore have, in theory, the controlling stake over her mother and uncle Santo, who own 20 and 30 percent respectively. No one was able to tell me how that would actually affect the running of the business: "This is a family issue, and it's still being discussed by the family," said one of the Versace press officers, when I pressed her on the point. And perhaps it was a near-unanswerable question: because how could you even begin to disentangle the history that lies behind that inheritance? What does seem clear, however, was that Gianni's primary relationship was with his sister. True, he often quarreled with Donatella (to such a degree that they had been estranged at times in the year before his murder), yet he absolutely adored her; "this naughty little sister who understood her big brother like no one else did when they were growing up in Calabria," said Rupert Everett to me, "the pair of them dreaming the dream that they were going to make it, and then they did, they really did. So there was this complete commitment to each other—almost like a marriage. Nobody could live up to Gianni for her." (As for Gianni's feelings for his sister: in a *Vanity Fair* article published just before his death, he remarked, "I think if I were to marry I would look for a girl like Donatella. Our friendship was from when we were children. We were always together.")

How, I asked her, six and a half years after Gianni's murder, would she describe her brother? "He was my protector, my friend, everything," she said. Did she feel alone still? "Yes," she replied, and then was silent again, looking as if she would prefer to disappear into the vast electric green python bag, gaping open by her side.

Poor Donatella: so expertly put together—from her astonishing sweep of hair to her taut tanned midriff to her fabulous lavender-varnished toenails—yet for all that audacious facade, she had a truly haunted look about her; not constantly, but every so often, as if a black cloud had swept over her sun-bronzed face. And when she did talk about her brother's death, I wondered whether she was also talking about herself; for there might be some truth in the cliché that when Gianni died, something in her died, too. "I never believe that Gianni is happier where he is," said Donatella, looking briefly upward from her python bag. "He would be much happier to still be here. He didn't want to die. He was killed brutally. My world stopped that second—and stopped for a while. I was obsessed with seeing my brother's body, so I went to Miami, and that was done. It was terrible. People say about the dead, "they're at peace." He didn't look that way. He was scared—the look on his face was one of terror. I realized that the world was not a good place. The world is a very bad place. You have to protect yourself from it."

So here was Donatella, in this bad place, retreating from it, yet still ruling her empire, "like being locked inside a Medici court," according to one of her friends; surrounded by bodyguards who looked like camp Hollywood bit actors; trying to make everything work, trying to fit it all together—pearl lipgloss and black cashmere and Tiffany diamonds, all wrapped round a broken heart. What hard work this project must have been; how exhausting an undertaking. No wonder she looked distracted; no wonder our conversation about Versace beauty products began to seem more than a little surreal (not that it's an unimportant subject: over £10 million of the label's products are sold every year in the UK alone; a big chunk of a vital market, because in the luxury fashion business, lipstick and perfume are far more than small frivolities, but the backbone of success). Here, for the record, was the Donatella creed. "The most important thing about being beautiful is a woman's skin. I always take a shower and use a nut oil on my body. I nourish my body and my face." When it comes to makeup, "I always make sure that the skin shows through—you should never cover your skin with makeup, that's the worst thing to do . . . I never use foundation, never. I use blusher, no powder. I like my skin to be shiny." Above all, she said, "it's important to smile with your eyes. Don't be afraid of a few wrinkles around your eyes . . ." But when she spoke, she was not smiling; the basilisk stare was unbroken.

It is, I think, safe to say that Donatella gives out very mixed messages: but to do otherwise would, perhaps, constitute a failure in her role as the grandest of Italian fashion divas. If

Versace was built on Gianni's ability to give a new spin to old ideas—classical motifs mixed up with the baroque; the Renaissance colliding with punk—then Donatella has always added even more to the mix. (As Rupert Everett observed, "She's not one thing or the other—she's a whole range of things. She's brash, but she's also discreet; she's vulnerable, but she's also very tough. She has so many different sides to her that she remains endlessly fascinating.") Presumably this was also why she could get away with telling me first that she was a Catholic, and then in the next breath announce herself as an atheist; that the fashion world would be looking for something "revolutionary" in the coming months, at the same time as admitting that "people are afraid in this economy, so we don't want to risk anything."

And these apparent contradictions reflect the clashing colors and prints that have become so associated with Versace style: those glorious pinks and yellows and hydrangea blues that could all go so horribly wrong, yet somehow look luscious and celebratory when Donatella puts them together. ("Beautiful, strong, passionate," she says, "the way Versace prints have always been.") So despite the undeniable strangeness of my meeting with Donatella, in retrospect, it makes a curious sort of sense. When I asked her what words she would use to describe herself, she came up with only one: "unpredictable." A little later, she said also that she was "very fragile . . . Every strong person is also insecure. Sometimes loudness and strength covers insecurity."

As to what else was covered up: well, Donatella's age remains mysterious (forty-five, officially, when I interviewed her, but her date of birth has previously been given as 1955). And she seemed reluctant to talk about her father (rarely mentioned in the Versace mythology; sometimes referred to as "a poet," elsewhere as much involved in running his coal business in southern Italy). She preferred, instead, to concentrate on her mother, Francesca, a seamstress who Donatella described as "a very strong woman—she worked all the time, she gave us so many good values. She was a very strict woman—I adored her." As a result, continued Donatella, she has raised her own children in the same way. "I am very strict about certain things . . . I have very old-fashioned values, about honesty. They have freedom if they know how to use it, and no freedom if they don't."

Would Allegra be free to choose whether or not to go into the family business that is her inheritance? "That's up to her," said Donatella, looking fierce. "She is interested in drama and business." It sounded like the perfect qualifications for a Versace successor.

Not that Donatella showed any sign of stepping down—"It seems a bit early to be speaking of successors," she said, "I don't plan to go anytime soon"; and it's hard to imagine the Versace family ever making way for an outsider. "I love the way every now and again I see a look of Gianni flash across Allegra's face," said Donatella. "I see him in her eyes when she tries to tackle a problem." And though she described herself as fragile—looked it, too—I came away in no doubt that Donatella had a robust inbuilt strength: the sort that stopped her from crying in public when her brother was murdered. "I had to keep everything going for the children, I had to keep up the company," she said. "I couldn't cry, because the cameras were always on me." As she spoke, I could see why she had become such an icon of survival, recognized by women from Moscow to Michigan; her face on T-shirts and makeup bags; better than Barbie, because here was a doll with a beating heart.

Even so, it remains impossible to reduce Donatella to a neat equation: hard on the outside, soft on the inside (or is it vice versa?); darkness mixed with light; the woman in black hard at work on making escapist fantasies out of turquoise georgette. She's far more complicated than that; far more *difficult*. When I asked her whether she felt she had achieved the right balance between work and motherhood, she said, fierce again, "That balance doesn't exist. We are all unbalanced."

And it's those words that I remembered, as I saw my final glimpse of Donatella, after the interview was over. There she was, this woman in the color of mourning, walking away across the courtyard, away from her dead brother's portrait, and she seemed almost out of kilter for an instant, as if her heels were too high, as if the unthinkable might happen, and she would fall. But then she righted herself, and kept on walking, faster now; faster than before.

13

Bella's Sweater

"Freud all his life set store on a neat appearance, and, indeed,
stressed its close connection with self-respect . . . When his
tailor was told that Freud was one of the cleverest men in the
hospital Freud commented 'the good opinion of my tailor
matters to me as much as that of my Professor.' "

Ernest Jones, *Sigmund Freud: Life and Work*

EVERYBODY NEEDS a favorite sweater—one to wear on gray
days, or to lift the spirits in times of dreary distress—and mine
is in plain black wool, unadorned aside from the white
embroidered handwriting on the front declaring "Je t'aime
Jane" and "Gainsbourg is God" on the back. As a matter of
fact, I don't love Jane, nor do I believe that Gainsbourg is a
deity; but I do love the sweater, because it reminds me of its
designer, Bella Freud, who gave it to me two years ago.

I can't remember exactly when I first met Bella, properly, but
I think it was a year or so after my sister died, when I was
working at *Vogue*. I already knew Bella to be a fashionable
west London designer, the epitome of gamine Notting Hill
cool, so whenever I came across her, at parties or fashion
shows, I felt a kind of wariness, at the same time as admiring
the way she looked (usually in pin-striped tailored trousers of
her own making, high wedge-heeled sandals, and one of her

trademark sweaters). I knew that she had modeled for her father, the artist Lucian Freud, who has been quoted as saying, "I paint people, not because of what they are like, not exactly in spite of what they are like, but how they happen to be." But Bella seemed to me to look as if she knew exactly how she *wanted* to be: which sounds simple, but isn't; it's a rare gift to be able to dress entirely as yourself, rather than an emulation of anyone else. I knew, too, that Bella was the same age as me, and that her younger sister, the novelist Esther Freud, was the same age as Ruth would have been; and when I saw them together, occasionally, it was clear that they had an unusually close, comradely relationship, as Ruth and I had had; and I felt a pang of envy, mixed in with the grief for what I had lost.

So the beginnings of our friendship were not entirely auspicious (though the fault was all on my side), but gradually, we began to get to know each other. Once, at a magazine shoot, she told me that we had something in common, in that our surnames were constantly misspelled. "I've just received a fax addressed to Miss Fraud," she said, "and I regularly get letters sent to Miss Fiend." She did not allude to the fact that as the great-granddaughter of Sigmund Freud, and Lucian Freud's daughter, she had one of the most famous surnames in the world, but I did, at least obliquely.

"A Freudian slip of the pen?" I said, and she had the good grace to laugh, delightedly, as if no one had come up with this unimaginative line before.

"I can never remember anything about my childhood," she then said, in tacit acknowledgement (as well as a gentle refutation) of her great-grandfather's famous exposition that the past, and our memory of it, governs both the conscious and unconscious decisions that we make in adult life. "But I do remember clothes: I remember every button I've used on every jacket I've ever designed, since my first collection in 1990."

Afterward, prompted by her remark, I looked up a passage from Sigmund Freud's *The Interpretation of Dreams* (a book I had read after my sister's death, when I was dreaming of her constantly), in which he revealed himself to be as intrigued by the meaning of buttons, and different aspects of female clothing, as he was about other clues to the workings of the unconscious. Freud described how one of his patients told him about a visit she had paid to a friend the day before. "She was invited to take off her jacket and declined with the words: "No thanks, it's not worthwhile, I have to go soon." As she tells me this, it occurs to me that while we were engaged in the work of analysis the previous day, she suddenly grasped at her jacket, where a button had come undone. It is as though she wanted to say, 'Please don't look, it's not worthwhile.'" Perhaps, continued Freud, we should "recall how frequently the smaller hemispheres of the female body stand in—as opposite and substitute—for the large ones in allusions and dreams."

And it occurred to me that Bella, like her great-grandfather (and her father, who had painted her both dressed and undressed), would understand that clothes carried a multitude of different messages; but she might also be infuriated by the assertion that those messages were always open to elucidation or decoding. (Why, for example, was Sigmund Freud so insistent on the specific sexual symbolism of clothes when they appeared in dreams? ". . . a woman's hat can very often be interpreted with certainty as a genital organ," he wrote in *The Interpretation of Dreams*, "and, moreover, as a *man's*. The same is true of an overcoat . . ." This seemed to me to be rather generalized; and anyway, why couldn't a hat simply be a hat? I found myself having arguments in my head with him; except Freud never said much in response to my objections to his hat/overcoat/penis theory, apart from "this is pure projection.") So I was interested, a year or so later, to see the immediate success of a simple black sweater Bella had designed (one that predates mine) with the message "Ginsberg is God" embroidered in white on the front, and "Godard is Dog" on the back.

Not long afterward, we met each other again, halfway down the staircase at a party: a big, intimidating affair, thrown by the art dealer Jay Jopling to celebrate Damien Hirst's latest opening at his gallery; a party lit by photographers' flashes, at a time when conceptual artists were jostling for position with fashion designers and supermodels in the pages of *Vogue*. I said to Bella that I was going home, that the party was all too much for me (the sort of event that can make you feel small, and also too large—neither thin enough nor rich enough nor famous enough to be there; discombobulated, shrinking and expanding in all the wrong places). But instead of leaving, we ended up retreating into a corner of the landing, talking for ages about that sweater; about what its cryptic message might mean, or whether it meant nothing at all. "It just came out of talking with some friends," said Bella, vaguely. "It seemed like the essence of an evocative moment." (Herr Doktor Freud would doubtless have been unconvinced by such resistance to interpretation; but I liked Bella's elusiveness, her refusal to be translated.)

By then, the sweater had already sold out—she'd only made fifty of them in the first place, and once Kate Moss had been photographed wearing one, the others had been snapped up immediately. But she offered to lend me hers, and I wore it the following week, to a book launch for a collection of short stories to which I'd contributed (as had Bella's sister, Esther, who sighed when she saw the sweater, and said, "I wanted one of those . . ."). I still didn't understand the Ginsberg/Godard reference, and nor did anyone else at the party: though practically every woman there (agents, authors and publishers of all ages) asked where she could buy the sweater. There was one person who didn't like it, who described Bella's sweater as "the worst form of fashion elitism," and when I came to her defense, I realized that I felt the beginnings of an alliance with her; that we might become friends.

Women make friends all the time, of course, but I hadn't, after Ruth's death (nor was I very communicative with my existing friends, despite their patience and kindness). In fact, to do so seemed almost a betrayal of my sister, who had been my best friend; though I was beginning to realize (slowly, clumsily) that Ruth would not have wanted me to be isolated without her; that friendship was one of the things that makes life worth living, and that life must be lived. (As for everything else that Ruth believed made life worth living: well, I knew already that her list included new shoes, new clothes, red lipstick; sweet peas and lavender flourishing in the back garden, and a freshly baked chocolate cake served with properly brewed Earl Grey tea.)

Anyway. I didn't say much of that to Bella—I didn't think about the origins of our friendship, either, except later, in retrospect—but we talked about clothes instead, swapping notes on our mothers' sixties caftans and miniskirts, because they'd both been so young when we were born. Bella told me about how she'd longed to look "normal" as a child: not only when she and her sister were taken by their mother on the hippy trail to Morocco (a journey fictionalized in Esther's first novel, *Hideous Kinky*); but afterward, too, when they were sent to a Rudolf Steiner school in Sussex. "All those lumpy hand-knits and dreary, hideous hemp," said Bella, "and I was longing for a V-necked gray school sweater."

I told her about how Ruth had coveted my blue gingham school uniform, and then that we'd hated our uniforms as teenagers; tried every means to subvert the rules. She told me about leaving school at sixteen—"as soon as I could get out"—and her move to London, where she found a job working for Vivienne Westwood in her shop, Seditionaries; and how she came back to work as a design assistant for Westwood, after a spell in Rome living with an Italian aristocrat named Prince Ruspoli, who happened to be more than thirty years older than she. We talked about *Vogue* and little black dresses; about white T-shirts and pinstripe trousers. Along the way, I discovered that her favorite sweater—a hand-knit with a dog and piratical cross-bones on the front—was one of her earliest designs; and that the dog was a portrait of a much-loved whippet, Pluto, drawn by her father for Bella's first company logo.

And then one day she told me the story of a mistake that had just been made about the Ginsberg sweater (a mixed message of the sort that her great-grandfather might have enjoyed analyzing): the actress Jane Birkin had misread it as "Gainsbourg is God," and taken it to refer to her former boyfriend, Serge Gainsbourg, the famous French singer and sex symbol. Jane had been in touch with Bella to ask if she could buy one, but they'd already sold out. "I've been thinking about it," said Bella to me, "and it would be great to make another limited edition, with 'Gainsbourg is God' on the back and 'Je t'aime Jane' on the front."

She said she was worried about how to sell a single piece of knitwear, instead of an entire collection; but I told her not to worry; that she didn't have to obey the unspoken laws of fashion that dictate how, and when, a designer should present his or her work; that she should do what she wanted, when she wanted, just as she'd done in the past. (After all, she'd already collaborated with John Malkovich to make three widely admired films as alternatives to more conventional catwalk shows.) She said she knew that, she just wanted to find out what other people thought. I said it didn't matter what anyone else thought, that she'd always been the one with the good ideas, right from the start.

I'm glad to say the Gainsbourg sweater sold out just as fast as its predecessor, as did a subsequent sweater, with "Love" written on the front, in swirly Jimi Hendrix–inspired psychedelic orange and pink. (I never got my hands on one of those, so I've borrowed Bella's, again, whenever the occasion arises.) And I'm still talking to her about clothes: about the T-shirt she's designed—with such touching, painstaking care—to raise money for the Lavender Trust (which is the breast-cancer charity I set up in memory of my sister); about what to wear when I went to Milan to interview Donatella Versace (she recommended tailoring; I ended up in jeans and the "Love" sweater); about the pleasures of rediscovering old clothes in the back of one's wardrobe or at the bottom of a chest of drawers (to be honest, I prefer discovering her old clothes to mine). I could write a long list of what we talked about in these conversations, but I think the short version will do better.

1. You can wear socks with open-toed wedge sandals, whatever you've been told to the contrary.

2. The perfect pair of dark trousers are, in her words, "straight, but not narrow; slouchy, but dapper, in a schoolboyish way." (That longed-for uniform, again.)

3. A complete face of makeup is usually a mistake; it makes you look like you're trying too hard.

4. Just because everyone else is wearing hippy-chic slip dresses and ribbon-trimmed cardigans doesn't mean you have to join in. ("I've always known what kind of clothes I liked," she says, "and I know what I'm good at doing. So when tailoring went out of fashion, I wasn't going to stop making jackets, just because everyone else had. But there was one point in my career when I was under incredible pressure to do what other people wanted—and I hated it, I said I'd never do that again, because there's always going to be someone who wants a tailored suit, and a marvelous shirt.")

5. You can wear stars and spots and stripes together.

6. You can also wear navy and brown together (well, she does; I'm not sure it does anything for me).

7. Round-necked T-shirts are usually better than the V-necked version. And cap-sleeved ones are more flattering than no sleeves, unless you have very slender arms.

8. Fashion doesn't need to be literal-minded (hence the Biba-ish rose-print on the Lavender Trust T-shirt, rather than a sprig of lavender; and the T-shirt comes in green as well as lilac).

9. Turning forty-three isn't so bad, after all.

I've left out the other stuff, the bits in the middle, by which I mean the usual conversations about anxiety and insecurity and the dread that can overtake you just before dawn—because clothes don't always cover everything, I do realize that . . . Although, I must say, it's surprising how far a cryptically worded message on a sweater will take you; and how meaning (though not of a traditionally Freudian kind) can be found in what is more often dismissed as the meaningless; or to be more precise, that kindness and affection and friendship can emerge out of what is usually labeled as frivolous froth.

One last thing: there's still something troubling me about Bella's great-grandfather, which I can't figure out. In Ernest Jones's authoritative biography of Freud, there is an intriguing reference, in the section on his personal life, to Freud's intense frustration at not being able to afford to give his fiancée a particular piece of jewelry: "a gold snake bangle (*eine goldene Schlange*) . . . It was only after three and a half years, at Christmas 1885, that he managed to procure her a silver one." Jones—a fellow psychoanalyst, as well as a friend and follower of Freud's—makes no attempt to interpret the golden *Schlange*, which seems a missed opportunity, particularly given that Freud had put such emphasis on snakes as "those most important symbols of the male organ" in *The Interpretation of Dreams*. Perhaps Jones felt that to make any further comment might have been impertinent; or was Freud's desire to buy his fiancée a golden snake bangle just too obvious to need any further explanation? (Their engagement was a long one—over four years—largely due to Freud's lack of money; thus he was frustrated, financially and sexually; and his desire for the wealth that would allow him to be with the woman he loved was neatly represented by the *goldene Schlange*.) It is also possible, I suppose, that the snake bangle existed on its own terms in Freud's mind—not subconsciously or consciously emblematic; not phallic or representing solvency—just a precious piece of jewelry that he really, really wanted his betrothed to have. Or maybe it could be both of those things, or something else entirely: revealing, yet also opaque.

So I ring Bella up to tell her that the snake bangle doesn't have to *necessarily* symbolize anything; it could just have been the essence of an evocative moment, and then I remember: she'd already taught me that.

This Much I Know . . .

1. Do not wear a denim jacket with jeans: too reminiscent of a denim two-piece or suit. (Try a differently colored cord jacket with your jeans instead.)

2. Avoid solid black shoes with very pale tights: the combination looks like pigs' trotters.

3. You do not need to be a teenager to wear Converse All-Stars on your feet.

4. You do need to be a teenager to wear a micro-miniskirt. (And now I'm over forty, I'm reluctant to expose my knees, let alone my thighs.)

5. The older you get, the more flattering it is to wear something soft around the neck. (Something feathery or furry, perhaps, but not real fur. Please.)

6. Take a good look at your shoulders before you go for halter necks or spaghetti straps.

7. The law of fashion says, what goes up, must come down. And vice versa. Long skirts will follow on from short; hemlines will rise and fall, with ceaseless regularity. So never fret about whether your dress length is in or out of fashion: just wear it, if you like it, and if it likes you.

8. There is such a thing as different shades of black, and I always discover them when I'm running late, and trying to find a black sweater to go with a pair of black trousers. They never ever match.

9. White shirts or T-shirts with black trousers? Not necessarily a better alternative to the mismatched black: can end up looking like a waitress, instead. Black T-shirt with white trousers; better, possibly (though more stressful when it comes to avoiding stains).

10. Sweaters or other tops with a deep, tightly ribbed band at the bottom are difficult to wear unless you have a flat or toned stomach. Believe me, I've tried, and failed to get around this. Ditto cropped tops, but that's obvious, isn't it?

11. Belted cardigans: a conspiracy against womankind? Just about the most unflattering of looks: unless you're Kate Moss, but then she looks good in everything, even ponchos and capes; even in lemon yellow with a hangover.

12. Feel free to ignore all of the above: clothes are about self-expression; sometimes about surprising oneself (like most people, I lead an ordinary life, but occasionally feel the need to wear something extraordinary). Except the denim two-piece. I feel quite strongly about the inadvisability of that.

14

Scarlet Women

> "Out of the ash
> I rise with my red hair
> And I eat men like air."
> Sylvia Plath, "Lady Lazarus"

> "She was my first love. I felt that if I could have married Little
> Red Riding Hood, I should have known perfect bliss."
> Charles Dickens, "A Christmas Tree"

I

I CAN'T REMEMBER what age I was when I first realized that my mother had red hair—and that her red hair set her apart in some way—but I think I was still very young; young enough, certainly, for it to seem magical, almost like a fairy tale.

It wasn't until my own sons were born with red hair that I realized the strangely medieval assumptions that are made about redheads. "Hot-tempered, I bet," other women would say to me, as they peered into the baby buggy, though neither of my children was unusually fiery; indeed, were usually sleeping peacefully when the comment was made. (And can a baby be fiery? They always seem too milky for that unlikely adjective.)

So I don't want to give the wrong impression here about my mother, who was no more inflammable than anyone else's mother; who in fact has more self-control than many others I have come across. Nevertheless, as a child, I knew my mother to be special; and even though every daughter knows her mother to be unique, mine was marked out by the crowning glory of her red hair; that and her red velvet trousers, which she wore when she danced to "Jumpin' Jack Flash." Not that they were simply party trousers: she wore them when she ran across the park, and on the beach, when she kicked her legs high in the air like a cancan dancer; and I'd like to think they were the thing that made me spot her on the television one day, when she was demonstrating against the Vietnam War, outside the American Embassy in Grosvenor Square; but to be honest, it was 1968 and our television was still black and white, though I did see her, and so did my sister, and we saw the policemen who led her away.

There is an assumption that redheads shouldn't wear red—that the shades would clash horribly—but actually, my mother's red velvet trousers always looked wonderful on her; though unfortunately, red doesn't seem to work so well on me. That's what I'm thinking, vaguely, as I remember her sixties trouser-power—thus exposing myself, again, as being hopelessly un-revolutionary. The trouble is, red has lost some of its ability to look shocking; or maybe it's just the idea that doesn't seem new anymore, after decades of jokes about reds under the beds, and the red flag flying over socialist town halls.

But for all that, red—the right red—can still seem peculiarly compelling, particularly at the margins of things; when its rarity is a reminder of old magic. You can sense this in Emily

Dickinson's note—written when she was making her white-clad retreat from the world: "Friday I tasted life. It was a vast morsel. A circus passed the house—still I feel the red in my mind." And Rosamond Lehmann describes its effect (literally) brilliantly in her novel *Invitation to the Waltz*, published in 1932, an era when respectable English girls were still supposed to wear sweet-pea pastels, so that it seems all the more remarkable for her heroine, Olivia, to be given a roll of flame-colored silk for her seventeenth birthday, to be made into a dress for her first dance: "Olivia considered serviceable dark-brown or navy-blue winters, holland and tussore summers; cream viyella blouses, white piqué tennis skirts; all plain, neat, subdued, unbecoming. The patches of color splashing one's wardrobe life history were as rare, now one came to think of it, as roses in December. Each one remained vivid in memory: isolated accidents, shocks of brightness: a crimson ribbon slotted through an early white party frock, exciting, evoking again the drop of blood of the fairy story piercing the cold, blank, startled snow, piercing her smooth mind indelibly, as she read, with sudden stain . . ."

If I were dark-haired, like Olivia, like my sister, I'd buy a red party dress (and Ruth had a wonderful one, made of vermilion silk, which I hope has been saved for her daughter: because even if Lola never wears the dress, she should see it, and touch it, and know that her dead mother was once a laughing girl who danced in it, while the rest of the party spun around her, like a Catherine wheel). But red dresses have a bad habit of turning me sallow; so I content myself with smaller, darker red treasures: the garnet earrings inherited from Auntie Lil, and a tiny garnet brooch that my mother bought as a present for her mother, when I was born, and which my grandmother then

gave to me on my twenty-first birthday. And I take pleasure in
ruby lipstick—the best remedy when feeling slightly off-color,
or in need of a quick boost to morale (which is odd, because it
could be seen as a slash or a wound to the face). Red toenails
are good for lifting the spirits, too, though more high-
maintenance than lipstick; but I gave up on long red fingernails
after becoming pregnant with my first son, which is not to say
that mothers cannot be red in tooth or claw, but personally, I
felt it was time to forsake the talons, and step aside from the
battle of the sexes. ("What a weapon is beauty!" declared the
defiantly unmarried and childless Coco Chanel, whose own
favorite shade of red lipstick, Rouge Coco, was both her
personal trademark and a signature for her company.)

Aside from a secret passion for glittery red toenails, I also
have a weakness for red party shoes; thus it makes perfect
sense to me that the producers of *The Wizard of Oz* decided to
make Dorothy's magical slippers in ruby, rather than the silver
of Frank Baum's original book. (I'm also intrigued by the
stories of subsequent intrigue and treachery, as film-
memorabilia collectors maneuvered to own Judy Garland's
ruby slippers; now said to be worth a million dollars, despite
the fact that more than one pair are in circulation, as up to
seven are rumored to have been unearthed in 1970 from the
dust of the tattered MGM wardrobe department.) As a child, I
loved the film, though I never coveted Dorothy's slippers,
never wanted to be in her shoes, for they had a wicked witch
attached to them. Later, as a teenager, I discovered red high
heels in second-hand shops, and claimed them as my own; but
my favorite-ever pair came brand-new in adulthood, from the
designer Christian Louboutin, whose trademark is always a
subversively red sole. These were made of cherry satin, with

vertiginously elegant stiletto heels; and it is a measure of my affection for our dog that I did not eject her from the house after she chewed the shoes to pieces, having ignored my husband's sturdy walking boots and the boys' unattractive sneakers in favor of mine, bought at vast expense not long after I'd started working for *Vogue*. (She was still a puppy at the time, and did not know any better, though I sometimes wonder if her destruction of the red shoes was some sort of message to me: that I should be sticking to gray Wellingtons instead, all the better for walking her in? Or did she sense something of an animal threat in them; or were they the canine equivalent of a red rag to a bull?) Since then, I've bought another Louboutin pair—so that I can still flash the red soles, when the occasion arises—though these new ones have lilac suede uppers; partly because all-out red seems too tempting to dogs, if not disaster.

That red might equally presage doom as celebration—a red alert, rather than a red-letter day or a red-carpet moment—becomes apparent in *A Dictionary of Superstitions*. This reports that red ribbons have long been seen as unlucky for lovers (as are letters written in red ink); and red flowers were also feared by some as an evil omen. But then there are more entries in the *Dictionary* listing red as protection against all manner of ills: in 1314, a physician claimed to have used a scarlet cloth to cure the King of England's son of smallpox; while as late as the nineteenth century, red garters—preferably stolen ones—were said to be a charm against rheumatism; and red ribbon was tied around the neck to stop nosebleeds.

Brewer's Dictionary of Phrase & Fable (my other favorite reference book) reveals further ambiguities in the uses and interpretation of red: "In heraldry it is said to signify magnanimity and fortitude; in liturgical use it is worn at certain seasons; and in popular folklore it is the color of magic." The last point is made evident in a passage from W. B. Yeats's *Fairy and Folk Tales of the Irish Peasantry*: "Red is the color of magic in every country, and has been so from the very earliest times. The caps of fairies and musicians are well-nigh always red." It was also held to be magical by the alchemists: one of the names given to the philosopher's stone was the "red tincture"—the mythical substance that would turn base metal into gold. Aside from its magical value, red was used in church decoration to symbolize martyrdom: specifically, according to *Brewer's*, "martyrdom for faith, charity and (in dresses) divine love." Similarly, the red hat was bestowed upon cardinals—and became a term for the office itself—and scarlet is still the color of certain official costumes worn by judges and religious and academic dignitaries. Yet, somewhat confusingly, it is the color associated with promiscuous women and adulteresses: the title of Nathaniel Hawthorne's novel *The Scarlet Letter* makes explicit the practice in Puritan New England of sewing a scarlet "A" for adulteress onto the transgressor's dress. And the biblical origin of the scarlet woman as whore is nowhere more vivid than in St. John the Evangelist's vision in chapter 17 of Revelation: "I saw a woman sit upon a scarlet colored beast, full of names of blasphemy, having seven heads and ten horns. And the woman was arrayed in purple and scarlet color, and decked with gold and precious stones and pearls, having a golden cup in her hand full of abominations and filthiness of her fornication: And upon her forehead was a name written, MYSTERY, BABYLON THE GREAT, THE MOTHER OF HARLOTS AND ABOMINATIONS OF THE EARTH. And I saw the woman drunken with the blood of the saints, and with the blood of the martyrs of Jesus: and when I saw her, I wondered with great admiration."

If one were in the mood for being reductive—which I am not—a claim might be constructed that red is acceptable when worn by men, as a sign of status (the cardinal, the judge, the king), yet not by women, in whom it signifies something come loose (almost literally, as if wearing red unleashes a dangerous red-hot desire). But surely the symbolism of red is more complex than that: for red as a mark of blood does not distinguish between men and women (it is what links us, what lies beneath our skin). And despite the blasphemous blood-drunken scarlet woman in St. John the Evangelist's vision of filth, elsewhere in the Bible the faithful are exhorted to partake of the blood of Christ (". . . for my flesh is meat indeed and my blood is drink indeed"); though I am still not quite sure what to make of the blood-soaked suffering of His crucifixion which is known as the Passion; a sacred meaning that has been lost to many of us, myself included, when we refer to the passionate.

Yet where do they lead, these holy threads of red, if not to ecstasy: spiritual ecstasy, expressed in the most physical of ways? Thus the bleeding red stigmata that have been said to appear on certain saintly people, corresponding to Christ's crucifixion wounds, were nearly always seen on holy women; some of whom also claimed to be a Bride of Christ, wearing a precious gold and jeweled ring visible to no others, though it occasionally appeared as a reddened or blood-stained circle on their wedding finger. St. Catherine of Siena is one of the most revered of these women: and whether or not one is a believer, her story remains extraordinary, with all the true authenticity of a parable; as revealing as Revelation. Born in

1347, she was the twenty-fifth child of a prosperous wool dyer (sadly, legend does not relate if her father used carmine or vermilion or indeed any form of red, for this was still among the most precious and difficult of dyes to work with). Catherine soon set herself apart from her family, spending her time in prayers and fasting. As a teenager, she refused to marry, cut off her golden hair, wore a hair shirt, and scourged herself until she bled; until at last she saw a vision of Christ, who placed a ring upon her finger, which remained invisible to everyone but her. Soon afterward, she went out into the world, where she nursed the sick and dying, caring for lepers and plague victims, when no one else would. She also made a practice of visiting the condemned in prison, and is famous for her attendance at the execution of a young man who had requested that she be with him at his death. "He asked me to make the sign of the cross over him," she wrote. "I stretched out his neck and bent down to him, reminding him of the blood of the Lamb. His lips kept murmuring only 'Jesus' and 'Catherine' and he was still murmuring when I received his head into my hands . . . my soul rested in peace and quiet, so aware of the fragrance of blood that I could not remove the blood which had splashed onto me." The blood on St. Catherine's hands was as sweet to her as it was to become foul to Lady Macbeth; elsewhere in her writings, a central theme is that of Christ's blood as the supreme sign and pledge of divine love ("Christ did not buy us with gold or silver or pearls or other precious stones, but with his own precious blood"); though when she received her stigmata, she prayed that they should remain invisible, like her wedding ring. The red wounds were said, at last, to appear on her body when she died of a mysterious illness after terrible suffering, at the age of thirty-three. Afterward, her head was cut off and taken to her native Siena, where it remains on display, mummified, in a reliquary at the San Domenico church; while her body—believed to be incorruptible, when it was reexamined, fifty years after her death—was buried beneath the altar of the church of Santa Maria sopra Minerva in Rome. Canonized in 1461, St. Catherine is the patron saint of fire prevention (I cannot discover why this is the case; though I presume it might have something to do with the flames of her faith—her trust in God's holy fire, as opposed to earthly passions or hellfire). Her principal iconographical emblems are the ring, the cross, the lily, and the stigmata: the red and the white; the agony and the ecstasy.

II

As a daughter of radical atheists (though subsequently, my father has returned to some of the rituals of Judaism; and I have always been close to my mother's older brother and his wife, both of whom are devout Catholics), I did not receive the kind of religious education that might have taught me that red could be both sacred and profane. But red as a harbinger of disaster was never clearer than in the books I read as a child, and have come back to in adulthood. First, there was Little Red Riding Hood ("Grandmother, what big teeth you have." "All the better to gobble you up!"); and Briar Rose, who pricked her finger on a spindle, the drop of red blood turning her into the cursed Sleeping Beauty, imprisoned for a hundred years until her prince could come. And then, more dreadful, was Hans Christian Andersen's story "The Red Shoes," in which a little girl named Karen is given a pair of red shoes on the day that her mother is buried. As she walks behind the coffin of straw, Karen is rescued by a grand old woman, who takes her in and gives her new clothes to wear, and burns the shoes. But Karen still wishes she had another pair, particularly after she sees a young princess, dressed all in white, aside from her beautiful red kidskin shoes. By the time Karen is old enough to be confirmed, the old woman is too blind to see properly, and does not realize that the girl has acquired a new pair of red shoes, an immodest color that she nevertheless wears to her first communion. Outside the church, Karen meets an old soldier with a long red beard, who places a curse on the shoes: thus, when the old woman is close to death, and Karen does not stay at home to nurse her, but goes out instead to a ball, the shoes grow onto her feet, and she is condemned to endless dancing. Her punishment seems complete when she dances across a graveyard, and sees an angel in long white robes, with wings that reach from his shoulders to the ground. " 'Dance you shall!' he said. 'Dance in your red shoes until you turn pale and cold!' "

Karen asks for mercy, but none is given, and she dances until her feet are bleeding. Such is her torment that when she finds the house where the executioner lives, she confesses to her sin, and then asks him to chop off her feet, which dance away into the forest in their devilish shoes. "And he carved wooden feet and crutches for her, taught her a hymn that sinners always sing, and she kissed the hand that had wielded the ax . . ." (At twenty-one, not long out of university, I dreamed one night of a friend of mine crucified by a red devil on a cross, and his feet had turned to wooden stumps, and I had to help him hobble away to safety; an embarrassingly florid Gothic nightmare that made no sense to me at the time, though I never forgot it; and now I wonder if it grew out of the Andersen tale, rather than any, more conventional, knowledge of Christianity.) Anyway, after her encounter with the executioner, Karen sets off on her wooden feet to church, but when she gets there, the red shoes are dancing in front of the door, preventing her from going inside; so she repents further, and takes an unpaid job in the parsonage. "All the children were very fond of her, but whenever they spoke of adornments or finery or being as lovely as a queen, she would shake her head." Finally, she is forgiven by the angel of God, and allowed into the church. "Her heart was so filled with sunlight, with peace and joy, that it burst. Her soul flew on the sunlight to God, and no one asked about the red shoes."

That Hans Christian Andersen was the son of a shoemaker simply adds to the macabre cruelty of his story; but the barest outline of his life makes it clear why his stories were as grim as the Brothers Grimm's, even though they were subsequently sweetened (and also mutilated) in translation. Born in 1805 in a provincial Danish town, he was a lonely, only child, ostracized by others as freakish, and left to his own devices, as he sewed dolls' clothes and played with his puppets. His paternal grandfather, a woodcarver, was jeered at in the town as a madman; and it was in the local lunatic asylum, where his grandmother worked in the spinning room, alongside other impoverished old women, that he heard the folktales that were to weave their way into his writing. In his memoir, *The Fairy Tale of My Life*, Andersen had not forgotten that early education: "The stories told by these old ladies, and the insane figures which I saw around me in the asylum, operated so powerfully upon me, that when it grew dark I scarcely dared go out of the house. I was therefore permitted, generally at sunset, to lie down in my parents' bed . . . here I lay in a waking dream as if the actual world did not concern me."

And yet he could not escape the actual world, or his place in it, or the fear that he might be following in the footsteps of his grandfather the lunatic. "One day . . . I heard the boys in the street shouting after him," wrote Andersen. "I hid myself behind a flight of steps in terror for I knew that I was of his flesh and blood." If life were a fairy tale, as the title of his memoir suggests, then there might be no better way to avoid those footsteps than to cut off one's feet; to sacrifice one's own flesh, in order to escape the legacy passed down by blood relatives.

His father the shoemaker had died when Hans was eleven; which is perhaps why soles are inextricably linked with souls in his stories; why the price that his Little Mermaid must pay for a witch's spell that gave her feet to walk on dry land is perpetual agony, as if she were treading on knives. And blood plays a central part in this tale, too, as does red: for the Little Mermaid is drawn from her ocean home first by the sun above the waves, "like a crimson flower from whose chalice all light streamed"; and she plants red flowers in her sea-garden, to remind her of this. Later, she makes a pact with a sea-witch: to gain the feet she needs to be reunited with the human prince she has fallen in love with, and to have the chance of gaining an immortal soul—for though they live for three hundred years, mermaids do not have souls, unless they marry a human—she will let the witch cut off her tongue in return for a magical potion containing the witch's own blood. Once she has feet, the newly mute Little Mermaid goes in search of her prince; but he does not love her as she loves him, and when he finds another bride, the Little Mermaid must die, unless she stabs him in the heart with a knife, and lets his blood drip on her feet, whereupon they will grow back into a tail. But she proves herself too good to kill him, and throws the knife into the sea, where "it looked as if drops of blood were trickling up from the water." For this she is rewarded by becoming one of the "daughters of the air"; rising up through the crimson clouds, on her way to "God's sun."

As far as I know, Freud never undertook a detailed psycho-analytic reading of Andersen, though he did make occasional reference to him—to his famous story "The Emperor's New Clothes" in *The Interpretation of Dreams*, in which Freud observes how typical is the dream of humiliating public nakedness (thus "the Emperor [is] the dreamer himself"); and also, equally briefly, in *The Uncanny*, where Andersen's stories are cited as evidence of Freud's somewhat surprising belief that fairy tales are not in the least uncanny. But it was the closer analysis of another troubled son, Little Hans, that was to form a cornerstone of Freud's theory of the Oedipus complex and castration anxiety; preoccupations that might also have been relevant to Hans Christian Andersen (the boy who had lain in a waking dream in his parents' bed), though I'm not entirely sure where God's sun and air's daughters would have fit into the theory.

III

I cannot have been the only teenage girl to come to the fire and Eyre of Charlotte Brontë hard on the heels of Hans Christian Andersen; and for their stories to chime, to feel as if they started from similar places, before going their separate ways. But if Andersen provides a visceral account of the blood that must be shed by those who have followed their hearts, or in punishment for devilish desires, and of the fiery torments endured in the name of love, both divine and otherwise, then there are different consequences arising out of Jane Eyre's red-blooded passion and rage, in a novel written in 1846, the year after "The Red Shoes" was first published. (I'd like to be able to say that I'd found some evidence that Charlotte Brontë was familiar with Andersen's work, but sadly there is none that I know of; though what is true is that his fairy tales were widely read after being translated into English in 1846, and it has also been suggested that she knew Little Red Riding Hood, and other fairy stories. Certainly, Jane Eyre hears "passages of love and adventure taken from old fairy tales and older ballads," told her on winter evenings by a servant, Bessie, while she irons lace frills and crimps nightcaps.)

I was talking about this recently to a friend—telling her that I'd been rereading *Jane Eyre* and Hans Christian Andersen, and wondering about the connections that one might make between them—and she said to me, "Why are you so interested?"

"Because it's interesting," I said.

"I'm not saying it's not interesting," she said, "but why does it interest you?"

I wasn't sure how to answer her then; but now I think that it has something to do with my mother, not least because she gave me my first copy of *Jane Eyre*. The novel's heroine is, of course, motherless, as was Charlotte Brontë (like Karen in "The Red Shoes," and the Little Mermaid); and when I came across all of these stories, as a child, I was already filled with anxiety that my mother would die, or disappear, or be kid-napped; almost as if her red hair had marked her out or made her vulnerable. Which may be why I felt a kind of unease when I read *Jane Eyre*, but also knew it to be powerful; for there were scenes within it—Jane as a child being locked in the red room; and later, mad Mrs. Rochester escaped from her secret room, and tearing up the wedding veil—that seemed somehow familiar, like remembering a nightmare. What is odd is that there is much about the novel, and its awkward, prickly heroine, that irritates me (and always has, which is why I've taken more straightforward pleasure in *I Capture the Castle* or *Cold Comfort Farm* or most of Nancy Mitford's novels). It's got a really weird ending, and very little in the way of jokes, and the men lurch between Gothic horror and sanctimonious priggishness, and Jane can be a bit of a prig, as well. But even so, I can't escape from that unsettling sense of recognition that accompanies *Jane Eyre* (which must be shared by innumerable other readers)—and I don't mean that I recognize myself in the novel, but I recognize something else in it, the secrets and the madness and the heroine who must learn to uncover her true self, as well as several others'.

That's what I'd try to explain to my friend, if ever she were to ask me again about why I was so interested in *Jane Eyre*; even though it might feel embarrassing to admit to such a thing; and even though I know the potential for further embarrassment is considerable, because people often behave in discomfiting and unlikely ways about the Brontës; claiming them as their own, apparently intent, like Mr. Mybug in *Cold Comfort Farm*, on proving to the world that they have dis-covered something of unique psychological insight. (And maybe that's part of what is intriguing about *Jane Eyre*—that its characters could make its readers behave out of character.) Nevertheless, at the risk of sounding Mr. Mybug–ish, it seems to me that there are all kinds of interesting suggestions contained within the novel about what it might mean to be a scarlet woman: which is possibly one of the reasons why it was a best seller from the start, and the subject of heated criticism for what some saw as its impropriety and corrupting power, so that Charlotte Brontë's admirers—led by Mrs. Gaskell, her friend and biographer (who nevertheless found something coarse in Jane Eyre)—were forever mounting defenses of the author's "purity." Mrs. Gaskell subsequently introduced a scarlet woman into *The Life of Charlotte Brontë*—almost as if in diversion, though also as part of her attempt to show that Charlotte, the angel in her father's parsonage, had been "forced to touch the pitch" by the corrupting presence of her debauched brother, Branwell (who, among other sins, was said to have had an illicit relationship with a married woman). The conflict has raged, in different forms, ever since (a battleground fought by feminist critics and psychoanalysts, Marxists and postmodernists, in which *Jane Eyre* has been claimed as wholly secular, or wholly puritan), perhaps because the novel itself is conflicted; just like its heroine, as is revealed close to the beginning of the book, during her incarceration in the red room. Jane is still a child in this early episode, an unloved and unhappy orphan living with her aunt, Mrs. Reed, and unkind cousins, in their family home of Gateshead Hall. After one of the cousins, a bullying boy, has thrown a book at Jane, her head is left bleeding; but when she flies back at him (in a different rush of blood to the head), her aunt orders that Jane be locked in the red room as punishment; and she narrowly avoids being tied down there by a servant's garters (a peculiarly evocative detail). Despite the fiery color of its walls and furnishings, it is a cold and silent place, usually unvisited by anyone in Gateshead Hall, aside from Mrs. Reed at rare intervals, who goes there only to inspect the contents of a secret drawer in the wardrobe, which contains her jewel casket and a miniature of her dead husband, Jane's uncle. The secret of the red room—"the spell which kept it so lonely in spite of its grandeur"—is that Mr. Reed had died in it nine years before, "and, since that day, a sense of dreary consecration had guarded it from frequent intrusion."

As darkness falls, Jane can see "subdued, broken reflections" in the glossy panels of the wardrobe; and more reflections in a large looking glass. "All looked colder and darker in that visionary hollow than in reality; and the strange little figure there gazing at me, with a white face and arms specking the gloom, and glittering eyes of fear moving where all else was still, had the effect of a real spirit." Jane, like the Brontë children, has been told enough local folk tales to see the reflection as "like one of the tiny phantoms, half fairy, half imp . . . represented as coming out of lone, ferny dells in moors . . ." Fear and superstition do not yet overcome her ("my blood was still warm"); but as time passes, Jane becomes more frightened, until she is sure that her uncle's ghost is returning to the room. Hearing her screams of fear, her aunt orders that Jane's punishment be increased: "you will now stay here an hour longer, and it is only on condition of perfect submission and stillness that I shall liberate you then."

Jane has a fit, and lapses into unconsciousness, "waking up with a feeling as if I had a frightful nightmare, and seeing before me a terrible red glare . . ." Afterward, when she reveals herself to her aunt as defiant, rather than submissive, Jane feels "the strangest sense of freedom, of triumph . . . as if an invisible bond had burst." Her pulses throb—she is red-blooded, again—but after a time, her fire is quenched: "A ridge of lighted heath, alive, glancing, devouring, would have been a meet emblem of my mind when I accused and menaced Mrs. Reed: the same ridge, black and blasted after the flames are dead, would have represented as meetly my subsequent condition . . ."

She is dispatched to boarding school—Lowood, a fictionalized version of the Clergy Daughters' School at Cowan Bridge, where Charlotte Brontë was sent at eight, and suffered the harsh regime that contributed to the deaths of her two older sisters, Maria and Elizabeth. In the novel, Jane sees the cruelty meted out to another pupil, Helen Burns (later identified by Mrs. Gaskell as being based on Maria Brontë), who is beaten on the neck with a bunch of twigs, yet despite her name shows none of Jane's burning indignation; who endures her flogging, and other sufferings, like a Christian martyr or a medieval saint, showing the perfect submission demanded of Jane by her aunt (and the final submission of the heroine of Andersen's "The Red Shoes"). "I could not comprehend this doctrine of endurance," says Jane of her companion, though she admits that Helen "might be right, and I wrong."

Jane has no choice but to undergo the miseries of Lowood, along with Helen and the other famished pupils. Their plain brown dresses and gray cloaks are insufficient to protect them from the severe cold; their ungloved hands become covered in chilblains, as do their feet, for they have no boots, so that the snow gets into their shoes, and melts there. Such is the reddened inflammation of Jane's feet that she suffers "the torture of thrusting the swelled, raw, and stiff toes into my shoes in the morning." But all this is of no account to the school's founder, Mr. Brocklehurst, who believes that their suffering is a good reminder of "the torments of the martyrs"; and also of the fate of wicked children who will go to hell, to burn forever in a pit of fire, as he tells Jane Eyre at his first meeting with her. ("What a face he had," she says, "what a great nose! and what a mouth! and what large prominent teeth!" As Professor Michael Mason observes, in his notes to the Penguin edition of *Jane Eyre*, "The sequence of exclamations perhaps indicates Jane's familiarity with the Little Red Riding Hood tale.") Thus if salvation can be found in pain and denial and control, then Mr. Brocklehurst detects something more devilish in a pupil with an abundance of naturally curly red hair: "—*what* is that girl with curled hair? Red hair, ma'am, curled—curled all over?"

The saintly Helen Burns's faith is not of the same kind as Mr. Brocklehurst's creed, for she believes that all will be saved, rather than consumed in flames. "Where is God? What is God?" asks Jane of Helen, in a crisis of faith. "My Maker and yours; who will never destroy what he created," replies Helen, just before she dies of consumption. Her pale goodness is, presumably, to be admired; though as a reader, it is hard to see it as any match for Jane Eyre's rebellious streak—a defiance that carries her safely into womanhood, unlike Helen, who wastes away as a girl. But the darker figure of Bertha Mason, the mad Mrs. Rochester who looms over the second half of the novel, appears almost as a warning, of how defiance and passion mixed with bad blood might lead to the hell on earth that she inhabits, locked away from civilized society. "Ghosts are usually pale, Jane," says Mr. Rochester, after she has described the "discolored" face and rolling red eyes of the specter that has stolen into her bedroom. "This, sir, was purple: the lips were swelled and dark; the brow furrowed; the black eye-brows widely raised over the blood-shot eyes."

Later, after Jane's abandoned wedding to Mr. Rochester, when he finally allows her into the room on the upper floors of Thornfield Hall, where he has kept his first wife prisoner, Bertha is described as more animal than human: "the clothed hyena rose up, and stood tall on its hind feet" (like the wolf in "Red Riding Hood"). Rochester binds Bertha to her chair (with rope, not garters), and then declares Jane to be "so grave and quiet at the mouth of hell . . ." And it is a kind of death; as if Bertha really was the Gothic "Vampyre" who has somehow done to Jane what she already tried to do in an earlier attack on her own brother, biting his arm and shoulder ("She sucked the blood: she said she'd drain my heart").

This bloodless, frozen Jane—"ice and rock," in Mr. Rochester's words—refuses to become a scarlet woman; will not be his mistress, given that she cannot marry him. Yet it is Rochester—who was prepared first to make a bigamous marriage, and then to have an adulterous relationship with Jane—who describes Bertha as "a wife at once intemperate and unchaste . . . no professed harlot ever had a fouler vocabulary than she . . ." That Rochester believes Bertha to be a scarlet woman is made explicit when he confesses everything to Jane, in the aftermath of their disastrous wedding day. "When I think of the thing . . . hanging its black and scarlet visage over the nest of my dove, my blood curdles—"

But it is the fire kindled by the scarlet woman that finally brings Rochester and Jane back together again; for Thornfield Hall is burned to the ground by Bertha, after she has set alight the bed that Jane Eyre once slept in, and she kills herself by leaping from the roof ("dead as the stones on which her brains and blood were scattered," reports a witness). As his house falls in ruins around him, Rochester is left maimed and blinded; yet Jane returns to him—"in the flesh? My living Jane?" he asks, incredulously; to which she replies, "I am not cold like a corpse, nor vacant like air, am I?"

As for Bertha Mason: there could be no more heartbreaking imagination of her life—both before the doomed marriage to Rochester, and afterward—than in Jean Rhys's *Wide Sargasso Sea*, written in 1966 (and yes, I found it on my mother's bookshelves, and read it, secretly). It is a novel that gives the first Mrs. Rochester a voice—a woman, not an animal—and she describes a red dress, hanging in a dark cupboard in her prison-room, but still "the color of fire and sunset." Holding the dress up against herself, she asks, "Does it make me look intemperate or unchaste?" Receiving no answer, she lets the dress fall to the floor: "it was as if the fire had spread across the room. It was beautiful and it reminded me of something I must do."

We already know the something she must do; we already know the ending to her story, but it is no less powerful for that. The scarlet woman finds the key to the locked door, and makes her escape; the phoenix rises from the ashes.

Which brings me all the way back to my mother again—a scarlet woman of her own making, escaping from her devoutly Christian parents, who disapproved of her politics (too radical) and her early love affairs (too passionate, for sex before marriage was simply beyond the pale). It was not that she was brazen—there was no trace in her of the famous Mae West quip, "I used to be Snow White, but I drifted"—but she has lived according to her beliefs. As a friend of mine has said of my mother, "She didn't just wear the T-shirt, she was out on the streets." (That the streets he referred to were those of sixties revolutionary politics, as opposed to those used for prostitution in red-light districts, is, perhaps, another indication of the semantic confusion that can become attached to a woman in red.)

And despite all her repudiation of the nuns who educated her at a convent school, there was something of the Crusader in my mother; and perhaps never more so than when she wore the red ribbon denoting allegiance with and support of people with AIDS. For my mother, as ever, it was more than just a badge. After her divorce from my father, she had been reunited with a man she had loved as a teenager (and my father, too, had rediscovered a girl he had known in his youth). He was a hemophiliac who had become a leading hematologist; a blood doctor who had become infected with AIDS. His first wife had already died of AIDS, having contracted the virus from him; he was sick and he was suffering when my mother married him. At the time, both my sister and I expressed our fears about their relationship, as did many of my mother's friends and relatives. But what I could not see then, though I do see now, is that she loved him; she truly loved him, and she followed her heart, expressed her desire, in defiance of everyone else's advice; undaunted by their disapproval in a way that seems admirable to me today, though foolhardy then.

After their marriage, she moved to live with him in New York, and though we were not estranged, there was a separation that had not been there before. We talked, yet much remained unspoken. Once, she told me that I was behaving irrationally about HIV; I said that I was not, that I could not be, after one of my best friends had died of AIDS. But what was true was that I felt a kind of superstitious fear, that related to blood, rather than an unseen virus; and my usually robust sister had developed a heightened phobia about blood—it made her feel faint; once, after she cut herself badly, she did faint; and she had a horror of seeing blood again. And somehow, everything had got confused and messed up and impossible to resolve; but when it came down to it, one thing remained clear. I didn't want my mother to die, and it seemed to me that she might.

As it turned out, it wasn't my mother who died. In rapid succession came the deaths of her parents, and then her husband, and soon afterward, her daughter. (When people say, life isn't like a fairy tale, they are perhaps forgetting that fairy tales reflect the savagery and cruelty and astonishments of life.) My mother's suffering was unbearable, and yet she bore it. There was nothing else to do, and somehow, she endured the pain; did not give way to black despair, and slowly, very slowly, found joy in the life she had left, as well. Her red hair is faded now to a soft gold, and she no longer wears red trousers, or indeed anything red at all. But she remains brave-hearted, my mother, and true to herself, and to others, in a way that very few of us are. And despite all that has passed between us (not least, the secretive, scandalous guilt of being survivors, amid so much death), we still love each other, because the bloodlines are unbroken; because the threads that bind us together are stronger than before.

How to Wear Red Lipstick (The Gospel According to Chanel)

1. One woman's flattering shade of red is another's unfortunate orangey mistake; so be prepared to experiment.
2. According to Dominique Moncourtois (the exceedingly

expert International Director of Make-Up Creation for Chanel), different nationalities need different shades of red. Hence, he designed "London Bus Red" to suit the English, rather than the French. "This color is especially for the light in your country," says Monsieur Moncourtois, "and for the English complexion. It's quite sophisticated, and feminine as well as sexy. And it's different from the French red, which has a hint of blue in it—like the red in the French flag. London red has a hint of gold instead."

3. M. Moncourtois has more detailed advice, as well. "If you're very pale, or very blonde, it might be too much during the day," he says, "perhaps a little too aggressive, though it will look great in the evening, even so . . ."

4. Otherwise, disregard the traditional rules concerning the correct age to wear red lipstick. "You are never too old!" declares Monsieur Moncourtois. "I hate those foolish rules about age. Look at Diana Vreeland [the legendary editor of American *Vogue*]—she always wore red lipstick, it was part of what made her iconic. And it's the same for the young—red lipstick doesn't have to look vulgar, it's just a question of balance and attitude. If you're wearing red lipstick, then don't overdo the makeup on the eyes and cheeks: black mascara, transparent matte foundation, and red lipstick, perfectly applied—that's the most elegant look of all."

15

Charlotte Brontë's Ring

"It was a little thing with a veil of gossamer on its head . . . a fairy, and come from Elf-land, it said; and its errand was to make me happy: I must go with it out of the common world to a lonely place—such as the moon . . . I said I should like to go, but reminded it, as you did me, that I had no wings to fly.

'Oh,' returned the fairy, 'that does not signify! Here is a talisman will remove all difficulties'; and she held out a pretty gold ring. 'Put it,' she said, 'on the fourth finger of my left hand, and I am yours, and you are mine; and we shall leave earth, and make our own heaven yonder.' . . . The ring, Adele, is in my breeches-pocket, under the disguise of a sovereign: but I mean soon to change it to a ring again."

Charlotte Brontë, *Jane Eyre*

I

I HAVE TWO of my mother's rings, which she gave to me in my twenties, when the joints of her fingers were beginning to swell and stiffen with arthritis. Now my own knuckles are just starting to show the same signs of early arthritis, like my grandmother and mother before me, so that the rings won't come off; I'm stuck with them, which doesn't worry me too much, because I've been wearing them, quite happily, for years. The ring that I wear on the middle finger of my left hand is a single garnet, set in a gold clasp in the shape of two hands; the one on my right middle finger is also gold, and set with eight tiny coral-colored stones (two of them now lost, as was the single pearl that they surrounded). Both are Victorian, and given to my mother by her father not long before his death: a present to console her for the loss of her favorite ring, which had been handed down to her by her aunt Madge, her mother's oldest sister. I remember the ring—another very delicate Victorian gold band, so small that it would only fit someone as fine-boned as my mother—with a gold clasp in the shape of a leaf, containing three garnets, two smaller ones on either side of the middle stone.

When the ring was stolen from my mother in a burglary, she also lost the Victorian turquoise and silver pendant that Madge had given her as a child; but she did not lose the story told to her about the jewelry, precious heirlooms which had been handed down through the Balfour family. Madge—short for Marjorie—was the oldest of the three Balfour sisters: she was born in South Africa in 1897; then came Hope, born in 1904; and finally Patricia, my grandmother, in 1906. (There were three boys, as well, but all had died in infancy; hence the long gap between the births of Madge and Hope, when the baby boys were born.) I have a sepia photograph of the three girls together, posed in a Johannesburg studio; undated, but Madge looks about twelve or thirteen, standing smiling with her arms around her two little sisters; the picture taken, my mother thinks, just before Pat joined the other two girls at a Catholic convent boarding school (she was four years old when she was sent away to the school, run by nuns). All three girls are in elaborately frilled white cotton dresses, just below the knee, worn over dark stockings and flat Mary Jane shoes. They have white ribbons in their ringlets, and tiny lockets and crucifix necklaces, too small to make out the details. I cannot be sure if Madge is wearing the turquoise and silver pendant, or if she has a ring on her finger; nor can I see the color of her hair—but my mother has told me that her aunt was the only one of those three sisters to have flaming golden-red hair, like her father, William Balfour. (And Hope's daughter, Molly, has another story, which was that when Madge was lying ill in bed at the boarding school, with a high fever, she saw a bushfire burning in the distance, and one of the nuns said to her that she should look more closely at it, to remind her of the fires in which she would burn in hell.)

Until recently, I'd never asked why Madge had given her two most precious pieces of jewelry to my mother; but when I did ask, she told me details of the story that I'd never heard before. "We were very close when I was a child," she said, "maybe because Madge didn't have girls, and her two boys had gone to boarding school after their father had died in 1936. Everyone said I looked very like her—and neither of my brothers or her sons had inherited the red hair. And also, she knew that I was interested in English literature, as she was— she read voraciously, and always bought me books as presents. She gave me all the classics when I was young—books that I wouldn't otherwise have read, and she knew that it was partly due to her influence I was going to study literature at university. That's one of the reasons she gave me the ring, when I was a teenager."

"Why?" I said, confused.

"Because it was Charlotte Brontë's ring," said my mother. "Madge had given me the Brontë novels to read, and she knew

I loved them, and also, she said that I was the only one whose fingers were small enough for the ring to fit—her joints had been getting swollen . . ."

"Madge had Charlotte Brontë's ring?" I said, astounded; because all I knew of my mother's aunt was that she was an accomplished pianist and music teacher at a girls' school in South Africa; that she had been widowed young, and died of cancer just before I was born, when she was not yet old herself.

"Yes," said my mother. "I'm not sure exactly where the turquoise pendant came from, though I know it was a family heirloom, but the ring was definitely handed down through the Balfour family. Madge's father—my grandfather—had emigrated to South Africa as a young man, but his grandmother, your great-great-great-grandmother, was Clara Lucas Balfour, and she knew Charlotte Brontë."

"She knew Charlotte Brontë?" I said, stupidly; stupefied, because though I'd heard the occasional reference to Clara Lucas Balfour as a child, I hadn't always been listening properly.

"Well, that's what Madge told me," said my mother, "and she wasn't the sort of woman to lie."

"And who gave Madge the ring?" I said.

"I'm not entirely sure," said my mother. "I think it might have been one of the Balfour maiden aunts—Madge went to stay with them in their house in Oxford, on the Woodstock Road, in 1950, when they were already old ladies. Or it could have been Madge's father, my grandfather, William Hall Balfour, though everyone called him Bill. He went back to England in the First World War, when he was serving as a captain in the Royal Navy, and though his parents were dead by then, the Balfours were a huge family, and he would have visited all his brothers and sisters and cousins. Maybe one of them gave him the ring, and then he gave it to Madge, his eldest daughter."

She reminded me that one of Bill's younger sister's children, Sir Hugo Marshall, had been the relative that we were closest to when we were growing up in England, while the others had scattered abroad, and that Hugo had also been the one most interested in the Balfour family history; in fact, had drawn me a detailed family tree when I was a child, and sent me long, wonderfully colorful letters, about the Balfour past.

I've kept his letters, and the family tree, carefully hand-drawn on a big sheet of graph paper; so faded now that the printed grid has almost disappeared, though Hugo's writing remains clear. So after the conversation with my mother, I got everything out from the bottom drawer of my desk (an old mahogany Victorian desk that my mother had bought for me as a child, where I still write; where I am writing now), and tried to make sense of the names and the dates, matching the stories in the letters to the genealogy. And it did make sense (more sense than when I had first received them), but what also came alive for me, rereading the letters, was Hugo, who had died twenty years ago. I remembered the many visits we had made to his house, in Wiltshire: Murrell House, built at the beginning of the nineteenth century in golden stone, sur-rounded by a rambling, stepped garden of lawns and woods and secret places, overlooking the greenest valley I'd ever seen. He had returned to England with his wife, Susan, after retiring as Governor of Nigeria; a return which had coincided with my mother's arrival in England, and from the time she had become pregnant with me, shortly afterward, she went to Murrell House often, as a refuge, I think, which was probably why it seemed to me to be the calmest of places, and Hugo and Susan the kindest of relatives.

And by the time I was eight or nine, after many visits there, I had become certain that it was the house that C. S. Lewis described at the beginning of *The Lion, the Witch and the Wardrobe*: the house where Peter, Susan, Edmund and Lucy had been sent as evacuees during the war, because of the air raids ("ten miles from the nearest railway station and two miles from the nearest post office"). It had long corridors and unexpected staircases and doors, just like in the book ("the sort of house that you never seem to come to the end of . . ."); and I felt sure that eventually I would find the room with the wardrobe in it, which would lead me to Narnia. (But it was on one of those exploratory adventures that I found myself trapped, rather than liberated, unable to open a door that I had locked behind me; and after spending some time shouting out of the window—there being no wardrobe to provide entry to another world—Hugo had heard me, and rescued me by climbing up a ladder and through the window, after the lock proved impossible to shift.)

Anyway, as I sifted through the letters—dozens and dozens of pages, all neatly typed on an old-fashioned typewriter, where the keys sometimes jumped—I could hear his voice again, woven with the printed words, and also prompting my memory of the other stories that Hugo had told me about the Balfours. His mother, Cecil Mabel Balfour, had been my great-grandfather's younger sister, which made Hugo the first cousin of my grandmother, Pat, and also of Madge and Hope; though he always referred to my mother as his first cousin, too, and addressed me in each letter as "My dear cousin Justine." The letters are not dated, but his references to my replies suggest that I had started at secondary school (and that all, perhaps, was not well at home; which might have been why I had become so interested in my family's distant past, as opposed to its uncomfortable present). In one of his letters, he devoted eleven pages to describing his great-grandfather, James Balfour, and then an account of James's wife, Clara Lucas Balfour, and her successful career as a lecturer and writer (the author of dozens of now-forgotten Victorian books). But the letter also made clear that some of the family stories about James and Clara were not necessarily true.

"As an old man," wrote Hugo, describing James, "he used to spin a yarn to my mother and his other grandchildren (including your great-grandfather, William Hall Balfour), that he was present at the Battle of Trafalgar; that his ship was sunk under him; and that he swam with a sailor under each arm. At first sight it seems very improbable that he could have been at the Battle of Trafalgar for he would have been only just nine years old when that battle was fought on the 21st October, 1805. Yet there are authenticated cases of boys as young as seven going to sea during the Napoleonic Wars so that my great-grandfather's claim that he was at the battle could be true and, if he was there, it is possible that his ship was sunk under him; the last part of the story is a typical piece of Balfour embroidery.

"This story, true or not, is all we know of James' early life. We next come across him in September 1824 when, less than a month before his twenty-eighth birthday, he married Clara, a girl who was not yet sixteen. Tradition says that she ran away from school to marry him . . ."

Hugo was fascinated by the girl's past, and had spent a great deal of time unearthing records of birth, marriages and deaths, to try to uncover the truth of her parentage. Clara Lucas Balfour, he continued in his letter to me, was "the most interesting of our Balfour ancestors, but in some ways her early life is the most baffling . . . There is an oft-repeated family story that Clara's mother married, during the Napoleonic Wars, a French prisoner of war and that Clara was their only child. After the wars were over Clara's father revealed to her mother that he had a wife in France whom he had married before he became a prisoner of war. Whereupon Clara's mother said goodbye to him forever and set out to earn her own living and support her only daughter.

"There is nothing improbable about this story. We know that Clara was born in south Hampshire, where her mother presumably lived, during the Napoleonic Wars; it is a fact that there were, at that time, large numbers of French prisoners in that area, many of whom were on parole, lived in the community and mixed socially with their English neighbours . . . There is another interesting circumstance which adds weight to the story. Clara's full married name was Clara Lucas Balfour. Lucas was almost certainly a family name, a surname, and one of which she was proud and felt fully entitled to use; for although she would have had no part in choosing her own name, she certainly had a part in choosing the names of her children, and the second name of her two eldest sons, Arthur and John, was in both cases Lucas. Lucas, as well as being a fairly common English name, was the name of at least one distinguished French naval officer—Jean-Jacques Lucas—who was captain of the ship from which was fired the musket shot which mortally wounded Nelson at the Battle of Trafalgar."

It certainly seemed like a splendid and romantic story to me: my mother's great-grandfather, John Lucas Balfour, William's father, had been named after *his* French grandfather, a captain in the dramatic naval battle where James Balfour had survived drowning, against all the odds, when his ship had been sunk under him. And even if James Balfour hadn't actually swum to shore with a sailor under each arm, he had made it home from the Battle of Trafalgar, and lived on to finally woo, and wed, the daughter of the French officer under whose command Nelson had been shot.

Unfortunately, Hugo's letter went on to suggest another theory, less colorful and also less popular in the Balfour family, that Clara's father was the son of a prosperous Isle of Wight family; that he and her mother were, for some reason, separated, but that when she was four years old, her father took her away from her mother to live with his relatives. He quoted to me a biographical sketch written by Clara's daughter, Cecil Balfour, which described the four-year-old Clara as "gaily dressed, riding her pony, and losing no opportunity to show off her wonderful facility for reading almost every English book."

She was educated by a governess, continued Hugo, but at the age of nine, "a great change came over Clara's life, for her father died and her mother either claimed or was forced to take custody of her child. She was almost destitute and decided to move up to London where she managed to support herself and her child by doing needlework, work in which Clara soon had to join." In his letter, he included another excerpt from her daughter Cecil's biographical sketch: "What it must have been to that young child to be taken from all the pleasant surroundings of a large farm, and all the lavish attentions of well-to-do relatives and friends, and to have to sit at a table in a dull room, in a dull street and stitch, stitch, stitch from nine in the morning until eight o'clock at night, her only companion the pale, silent mother on whose life had fallen such a blight." And when Clara's mother did rouse herself out of silence, matters did not improve for the child: "her mother was a strict disciplinarian and when she heard that Clara had been reading while she worked, made her unpick the long seam she had sewn and do the work all over again."

Poor Clara: who was beginning to seem to me like a cross between the young Jane Eyre and Sylvia in *The Wolves of Willoughby Chase*. Nevertheless, like both those heroines, her fortitude carried her through, as did her talent for embroidery on white muslin which, said Hugo, "at that time fetched a high price, and her mother agreed to set aside the money made by this work to send Clara to school." After months of embroidering the material for fashionable muslin bridal gowns, Clara finally earned enough to be sent to a boarding school in Essex, where she later became, in Hugo's words, "a sort of Pupil-Teacher"; though not for very long, because in September 1824, at the age of fifteen, she married James Balfour.

They had seven children: the first, a boy, born dead in 1825; then Arthur Lucas, born in 1827, who killed himself when he was nineteen, having swallowed poisonous acid in a park close to his home in London; Cecil, their only daughter, born in 1829; John Lucas, my great-great-grandfather and Hugo's grandfather, born in 1831; another son who died at birth or soon after, in 1833; James, born in 1835; and finally another son, Jabez, in 1843. I already knew Jabez to be the black sheep of the family: when I was a child, my grandmother told me of the terrible disgrace he brought upon the Balfours. A former Liberal MP, he was sentenced to fourteen years' imprisonment for his part in a massive fraud, based upon his extensive business empire (which had also employed my grandmother's grandfather, John Lucas Balfour, who was Jabez's older brother; though she hastened to point out to me that he had been entirely innocent of Jabez's wrongdoings). "Jabez died in a third-class train carriage," my grandmother said, in a hushed voice, as if that were the final disgrace; worse, almost, than his flight from justice to Argentina, where he was finally arrested, and his subsequent return in ignominy to England, for a much-publicized trial in 1895, and incarceration in jail.

Hugo's letters went into some detail about all of Clara's children, and their children, too, who formed part of a sprawling and ambitious Victorian family; one of them became a colonel in the First World War, and was taken prisoner, according to Hugo, "at the fall of Kut in Mesopotamia." Another—Cecil's son Edward—became a Fellow of the Royal Geographical Society, "and must, I suppose," wrote Hugo, "have done some exploring, but he was still quite young, not yet twenty-four, when he died at Leopoldville in the Congo."

But most of what he wrote in his later letters to me concerned Jabez and John Lucas Balfour; the latter's horror when he learned of his younger brother's embezzlements; and Jabez's enormous wealth and complicated frauds. There was some more information, too, about their mother, Clara: she joined the Baptist Church, and became involved in the Temperance movement in 1837 (probably because of her husband James's heavy drinking; though she later managed to persuade him to take the Pledge, and he eventually became a minor official in the House of Commons). It was at about the same time, wrote Hugo, that Clara "took up literary work, writing tracts, magazine articles and short stories." She was talented and enterprising enough to be employed by the *London and Westminster Review*, and it was through her literary activities that she became acquainted with Thomas Carlyle, who wrote for the *Review*, and his wife, Jane; a friendship cemented by the fact that the Carlyles lived near the Balfours in Chelsea.

In 1841, continued Hugo, Clara embarked on a lecturing career, alongside her now flourishing activities as a novelist and writer: "at first mainly on Temperance subjects and mainly to mechanics' institutes, the forerunners of working men's clubs and technical institutes, but gradually her repertoire and her audiences expanded and she started to go outside London, so that by 1846 she was carrying out lecture tours to Birmingham and Liverpool. Thereafter almost every year for the best part of thirty years she made at least one and sometimes several long lecture tours which took her virtually all over England and to Ireland and Wales and probably to Scotland. At her prime she attracted very large audiences, sometimes lecturing to as many as two thousand people."

Clara died in 1878, at the age of sixty-nine, having published more than sixty books and long pamphlets, the year after she had been elected President of the British Women's Temperance League. James outlived her, until 1884, by which time Jabez was on his way to becoming the wealthy squire of Burcot House in Oxfordshire; both parents, therefore, were spared the shame of their youngest son's downfall. But nowhere in Hugo's letters to me was there any mention of Clara's possible association with Charlotte Brontë, nor her ring. When I pointed this out to my mother, she remained certain that the story had, in her words, "the ring of truth about it. Madge was a stickler for facts."

She suggested that I contacted Hugo's daughter, Janet

Cunliffe-Jones, who had inherited Murrell House after her parents' deaths, and shared her father's interest in family history; my mother also reminded me (for like her aunt Madge, she is a stickler for facts) that in 1984, Hugo had sent us a copy of Janet's dissertation on Clara Lucas Balfour, written as part of her master's degree at Liverpool University. So I rang Janet, and arranged to visit her and her husband, David, at Murrell House.

The date we agreed upon was a Monday—24 January 2005—and there had been several newspaper and radio stories reporting that this was, officially, the most depressing day of the year, quoting mathematical equations to prove the point (something to do with the long hours of darkness multiplied by the rising levels of debt after Christmas). But I felt nothing but excited anticipation as I drove, at dawn, west out of London; a light fall of snow turning the far reaches of the suburbs into something more magical (or it seemed that way to me, though perhaps I was primed to see the ordinary transformed). I'd already told Janet about the ring when we spoke on the telephone, and though cautious about making any further connection, she had remarked that there were two references to Charlotte Brontë in Clara's diaries; diaries that her father, Hugo, had given to Janet before his death.

"Will you remember the way to the house?" she'd added, at the end of our conversation.

"I think so," I said; though I wrote down her directions, anyway. As it turned out, I missed the country road that I was supposed to take, but I did, with a jolt, remember the narrow lane that led to the gates to Murrell House, and its stone entrance, which seemed unchanged in the eighteen or so years since I'd last visited there.

"You look just like your mother," said Janet, when she came with her husband to the front door. "I expect people say that to you all the time . . ."

Walking though the house, I felt a similar sense of recognition; as if this version of Murrell House was related to an older one I'd already known; yet the two were not quite the same. One wing of the house had been sold, so that the corridors ended in different places; and the ceilings were far lower than I remembered as a child, when they'd seemed almost as high as the sky. But the faded rose-patterned wallpaper was unchanged, and the wide curve of the stone staircase; and the upstairs rooms were still familiar, with their views over the valley, and on the wall beside the door that I'd locked myself behind was a map of Narnia. "Was that map always there?" I asked David, who is a retired scientist.

"I'm not sure," he said. "I think it might have belonged to one of our children when they were younger."

Over lunch, and afterward, we talked more about Clara Lucas Balfour and her children; about her friendship with Thomas Carlyle, who had been impressed by her pamphlet "Common Sense Versus Socialism" (common sense always triumphed, in Clara's world); and whose own, far more eminent works Clara had first come across at the *Westminster Review*. And why had her oldest son, Arthur, killed himself, and in such a horrible manner? (He was "poisoned by corrosive sublimate," according to his death certificate, having swallowed the acid in a public park close to his home in Paddington Green.) "He was probably mentally ill," said Janet, and quoted to me a letter that Clara had written after Arthur's death in 1847: "It is better that he should be in his grave than a madhouse . . . I am thankful that my poor boy has escaped the miseries of a madhouse, and reached a world where there is no cloud to dim the intellect."

This, presumably, was the same unshakable faith that allowed Clara to write dozens of religious tracts, some of which are listed at the back of the only book of hers that I possess, *Morning Dew Drops*. The latter was one of Clara's most popular publications—dedicated "To The Juveniles of the United Kingdom"—in which she covered everything from the history of the Temperance movement to the importance of reading. In my edition, Clara appears on the frontispiece in a black and white engraving, looking the very embodiment of Victorian prosperity and self-confidence, her hair arranged in elaborate, sausage-like ringlets, a lace handkerchief balanced precariously on top, like insufficient icing for a cake. It is hard to see in this portrait, or in the lengthy pages that follow, anything of the girl she once was, though there might be a glimpse in Chapter 20 of her past. "I once knew a little girl who used to be employed in needle-work from nine in the morning to nine at night," wrote Clara, before moving on to her usual exhortations to self-improvement. "She was allowed an hour for her dinner-time, and she contrived to read the History of England, to study English Grammar, and to pay some attention to Geography, and other useful things, during that hour. The knowledge that is gained with difficulty is always sure to be well remembered; and I have no doubt that this little girl's information and good sense on the subjects she studied with so much perseverance, were far superior to those of many children who have greater advantages but are not careful to improve them."

One might speculate that Clara's high moral standards were more or less impossible for her children to live up to; certainly,

Jabez seemed to go to the opposite extreme (in fact, as Hugo had observed in a letter to me, Clara had said of her youngest son, when he was still only five: "I certainly think that there is very much to fear as well as hope in his case. He will be either good or evil—there is nothing negative about him.") But though it's not always easy to warm to the pious author of *Morning Dew Drops*, I found it far more moving than I had expected when Janet showed me Clara's notebooks and diaries—which her father had inherited from his aunt Edith (my great-grandfather's sister, and one of the maiden aunts that Madge had visited in Oxford, a few years before I was born). The little leather-bound appointment books, in which she listed her lecture tours, or undated account books, where she noted her income and scribbled down addresses, are not a complete set, nor do they make it clear whether Clara actually met Charlotte Brontë, or whether she was referring to her simply as a subject for a lecture; but the name does appear, in Clara's tiny, inky handwriting, against entries for visits to Brighouse and Wakefield in Yorkshire. I'd prefer to believe otherwise, but I know that if they had actually become friends, the likelihood is that Brontë herself would have referred to it in a letter, and it seems almost impossible that Clara would have been given a ring by Charlotte Brontë without the occasion having come to light before now. Even so, as I sifted through Janet's papers, I did come across an intriguing description of Charlotte Brontë in Clara's book *Working Women of the Last Half Century* (first published in 1854): "Miss Brontë's wonderful eyes, and mobile face, full of animation, was most fascinating, and had a beauty of soul that mere prettiness can never boast."

And while there was no proof as to whether their paths had

crossed, I couldn't stop myself speculating: might they have been introduced at the Keighley Mechanics' Institute, perhaps, where Clara appeared as part of her tours, and the Brontës often visited, walking there from Haworth to borrow books from its lending library or, more occasionally, to see lectures? Or could it have been through Thomas and Jane Carlyle, loyal friends and supporters of Clara since 1840, who met Charlotte Brontë in London, after the success of *Jane Eyre*? There was nothing conclusive, though Janet pointed out to me another passage in Clara's writing that revealed she visited the Brontë parsonage in 1856, the year after Charlotte's death, when the Reverend Patrick Brontë was still alive, and living with Charlotte's widower, his curate, Arthur Bell Nicholls. Clara's visit took place the year before Mrs. Gaskell published *The Life of Charlotte Brontë*, the best-selling biography that turned the writer into a Victorian household saint; and also before the journey to Haworth had become such a regular pilgrimage for Brontë fans (and collectors of Brontë relics and memorabilia). Clara, infuriatingly, gives no indication in her description of the parsonage of the reason for her visit; though presumably she was already a keen proponent of the romantic Brontë myth. "No imagination," she wrote, imaginatively, "however great its gloomy grandeur, could invent a deeper tragedy than that of Haworth parsonage, or describe a nobler character than its heroine." Her visit to the parsonage, she continued, took place in the summer, "in the golden glory of the sunshine, when the purple heather in ripe bloom robed the barren wild in more than regal splendor, and every fleecy cloud that languidly floated over the clear expanse of summer sky, threw its dreamy-looking shadow on the soft slopes, or abrupt undulations of the moor, giving a tender beauty to a landscape that, when bereft of bloom or sunshine, must be utterly wild and stern. Yet even in these summer splendors, the extensive graveyard all round the lonely severe-looking house, the old gray church tower rising just above and a little below it, made it a melancholy-looking place. I pictured it when the autumnal mists would gather like the folds of a wet tent around it; when the winter snows lay for months; followed often by the keen east winds of spring sweeping sleet from the German ocean across this high and desolate tract of country."

Later that evening, after I'd driven back home to London, I rang my mother, to tell her about my visit to Murrell House. I'd seen some of Clara's papers, I said, but they were fragmentary—there were huge gaps, in fact, where Clara's writing, and life, had simply disappeared; in much the same way that her success as a Victorian writer has now been completely forgotten—so I couldn't give my mother any more information about her ring. "It's just a tiny little story, like that tiny little ring," said my mother, sounding uncharacteristically wistful, "but it meant so much to me . . ."

There was something in my mother's voice—the disappointment, I suppose, and also the resignation to loss—that made me determined to find out more; or at least, not to give up until I had tried looking in different places. (And no, I'm not a Tolkien fan, but you don't need to have read *The Lord of the Rings* to understand the powerful pull of a small band; in fact, Freud predates Tolkien on this matter, for in 1913, after his psychoanalytic movement had undergone schisms and dissidence, he presented a gold ring to each of the five men in an inner circle of his followers. One of them, Ernest Jones, had made the initial suggestion that "we form a small group of trustworthy analysts as a sort of 'Old Guard' around Freud";

Jones later reported, with boyish enthusiasm, that at the first meeting of this loyal secret council, their master "celebrated the event by presenting us each with an antique Greek intaglio from his collection which we then got mounted in a gold ring. Freud had long carried such a ring, a Greek Roman intaglio with the head of Jupiter.")

Anyway. I rang my mother's cousin Gordon, Madge's son, who still lives in Johannesburg, to ask him if he could provide any more details; and he said no, though he did remember his mother's trip to Oxford, to stay with her aunts on the Woodstock Road, and he thought it possible that she'd brought the ring back to South Africa. So then I started from the beginning again, talking to various Brontë experts, to ask what they thought of the story, and reading my way through volumes of Brontë books and letters and biographies, searching for a clue, for a scrap of information . . .

Except it was hard to know where to begin in the accretions of mythology that had grown up around the Brontë possessions, and what they had (or had not) worn; for there is something obscuring in the mass of speculation—and adoration—that surrounds Charlotte Brontë and her family. (As Lucasta Miller puts it in her insightful book, *The Brontë Myth*, "the veneration of Brontë relics would become integral to the cult"; a cult which was already in full swing by 1895, when a museum of Brontë relics had opened in Haworth, at the suggestion of the recently formed Brontë society.) Much of this interest was originally fueled by Mrs. Gaskell's *The Life of Charlotte Brontë*, which provided reams of intriguing domestic detail: for example, in her description of Patrick Brontë's allegedly volcanic attitude to what his wife and children wore. "Mr. Brontë wished to make his children hardy, and indifferent to the pleasures of eating and dress. In the latter he succeeded, as far as regarded his daughters; but he went at his object with unsparing earnestness of purpose. Mrs. Brontë's nurse told me that one day when the children had been out on the moors, and rain had come on, she thought their feet would be wet, and accordingly she rummaged out some colored boots which had been given to them by a friend—the Mr. Morgan, who married 'Cousin Jane,' she believes. These little pairs she ranged round the kitchen fire to warm; but, when the children came back, the boots were nowhere to be found; only a very strong odor of burnt leather was perceived. Mr. Brontë had come in and seen them; they were too gay and luxurious for his children, and would foster a love of dress; so he had put them into the fire. He spared nothing that offended his antique simplicity. Long before this, someone had given Mrs. Brontë a silk gown; either the make, the color, or the material, was not according to his notions of consistent propriety, and Mrs. Brontë in consequence never wore it. But, for all that, she kept it treasured up in her drawers, which were generally locked. One day, however, while in the kitchen, she remembered that she had left the key in her drawer, and, hearing Mr. Brontë up-stairs, she augured some ill to her dress, and, running up in haste, she found it cut into shreds."

It seems unlikely that Mr Brontë really did burn his children's shoes (though as Rebecca Fraser observes in her excellent biography of Charlotte Brontë, "Charlotte herself evidently believed the story of the dress being cut up and there seems to be some basis of truth in the story, as the maids confirm it"); but the gossipy anecdote was repeated over and over again, as were other, equally vivid stories told by Mrs.

Gaskell, and by those who followed her. It was Mrs. Gaskell who described the appearance of Miss Branwell, Patrick Brontë's sister-in-law, who came to care for the children after their mother had died. ("I have heard that Miss Branwell always went about the house in pattens, clicking up and down the stairs, from her dread of catching cold.") And it was Mrs. Gaskell, also, who reported on the rules of Cowan Bridge School, drawing parallels with Lowood, in *Jane Eyre*. "The pupils all appear in the same dress," she wrote in *The Life of Charlotte Brontë*, quoting from the school entrance rules. "They wear plain straw cottage bonnets, in summer white frocks on Sundays and nankeen on other days; in winter, purple stuff frocks, and purple cloth cloaks."

The more I read, the more I realized that I could spend several months engaged in collating the stories relating to the sisters' clothes and jewelry. I found myself scribbling endless and increasingly peculiar notes, cross-referring Mrs. Gaskell's description of the Cowan Bridge/Lowood school uniform with passages in *Jane Eyre*. ("You need not look at me in that way," Jane says to Mr. Rochester, having turned down his choice of "rich silk of the most brilliant amethyst dye, and a superb pink satin" for her trousseau, in favor of a more sober black satin and pearl-gray silk: "if you do, I'll wear nothing but my old Lowood frocks to the end of the chapter. I'll be married in this lilac gingham—you may make a dressing gown for yourself out of the pearl-gray silk, and an infinite series of waistcoats out of the black satin.") And then the fictional mention of the colored silks sent me back to Mrs. Gaskell again, but a different chapter, quoting one of Charlotte's letters from 1851, over three years after the successful publication of *Jane Eyre*, in which she appeared to reveal—to me, at any rate, in the grip of this fevered obsession—a touching uncertainty about what might be suitable material for her own clothes. ("I went to Hurst and Hall's for the bonnet, and got one which seemed grave and quiet there amongst all the splendors; but now it looks infinitely too gay with its pink lining. I saw some beautiful silks of pale sweet colors, but had not the spirit nor the means to launch out at the rate of five shillings per yard, and went and bought a black silk at three shillings after all. I rather regret this, because papa said he would have lent me a sovereign if he had known . . .")

Quite aside from the question of Charlotte's sartorial vacillations, I was also becoming very absorbed in Emily's disconcerting dress sense. Her first biographer, Mary Duclaux, interviewed Charlotte's oldest friend, Ellen Nussey, who reported on a shopping expedition to Bradford when Emily bought a most unusual dress fabric: "she chose a white stuff patterned with lilac thunder and lightning, to the scarcely-concealed horror of her more sober companions." There was similar dismay when she and Charlotte went on their first trip abroad, to study at a school in Brussels. "Emily had taken a fancy to the fashion," related Mrs. Gaskell, disapprovingly, "ugly and preposterous even during its reign, of gigot sleeves, and persisted on wearing them long after they were 'gone out.' Her petticoats, too, had not a curve or a wave in them, but hung down straight and long, clinging to her lank figure." So I drew up more cross-references: between Emily's liking for voluminous gigot sleeves with a mention of her mother's sleeves, in yet another Brontë biography; this one of Emily's brother, Branwell, by his contemporary Francis Leyland. (Leyland interviewed one of the maids at the Brontë parsonage, who confirmed the story of Patrick Brontë cutting up his wife's dress, but said that this was because he disliked its enormous sleeves. As to *why* the Reverend Brontë disliked the sleeves: Juliet Barker, the former curator of the Brontë Parsonage Museum, and author of a definitive book on the family, suggested to me that he may have seen them as a fire risk.)

It was during my conversation with Juliet Barker—who also, incidentally, said that the story of Emily's romantic thunder-and-lightning-print dress was most likely a fabrication—that I decided the notes were getting out of control; that I needed to get a grip: to put the sleeves and the silks to one side, and get back to the ring (a lost ring, admittedly, but nevertheless, the ring where this story had started). Juliet had made two helpful suggestions: first, that Clara Lucas Balfour might have bought the ring in one of the sales that took place after Charlotte Brontë's death; second, that even if she had not bought the ring, one of her children could have done so, knowing that their mother admired Charlotte Brontë. I therefore arranged to meet Juliet in Haworth, having taken her up on a generous offer to spend the day with me at the museum.

II

It was a gloomy February morning when I arrived in west Yorkshire: sufficiently dismal to have satisfied Clara Lucas Balfour's sense of dark foreboding and tragedy. I hadn't been here since my early twenties, when I was working as a reporter for the *Sunday Times*, and had discovered, much to my surprise, that a source I needed to interview about a Bradford news story turned out to live in Haworth (thus allowing me to get a quick infusion of Brontë nostalgia, after a lengthy conversation about race relations at the opposite end of the village).

The steep cobbled street that leads to the church and parsonage remained unchanged; and the crowded graveyard looked to me as melancholy as Clara Lucas Balfour had described it; though Juliet Barker—the best and briskest of companions in this place—said that it wasn't as depressing as all that; it was just that visitors came looking for sadness here. She whisked me away from the gravestones and into the parsonage, where she had worked as a curator from 1983 to 1989, and through to the library (in a later wing built by a vicar in the 1870s, after the Brontës were dead and gone), where the archives are carefully stored; where buried clues to the lost ring might be found.

There, Juliet suggested that I look through the catalogues of auctions that were held to sell off the Brontë relics: so I started with the sale that took place in 1898, after the death of Ellen Nussey, who had been Charlotte's lifelong correspondent. The catalogue listed a number of bracelets and rings, including a gold and hair brooch, believed to have been Charlotte Brontë's, and given to Ellen by Patrick Brontë after his daughter's death (memorial jewelry, made out of locks of hair cut from the corpse, was a popular, if macabre, form of Victorian remembrance). Several other gold rings were listed, but none of the lots referred specifically to a garnet ring; and I had no more luck with the catalogue for the sale that took place six weeks after Ellen Nussey's, which was selling off "The Museum of Brontë Relics" (a collection that had belonged to an enterprising Haworth local, Mr. Robinson Brown). But what was interesting, nevertheless, was the importance already attached to the Brontës' possessions, less than fifty years after Charlotte's death: "Silk Purse worked by Charlotte Brontë while in Brussels"; "Shell Cameo Brooch in gold frame, worn by Charlotte Brontë"; "Scent Bottle belonging to the Brontë family"; "Ivory Tatting Shuttle, Tape Measure, & nine pieces belonging to the Brontë family." By 1907, when Sotheby's advertised a further sale of Brontë relics, which had belonged to Charlotte's widower, Arthur Bell Nicholls, the Brontë Society was bidding against other equally keen collectors, all drawn by the prospect of the biggest cache of treasures so far. Nicholls had stayed on in Haworth as curate for another six years after his wife's death, living in the parsonage and helping care for his father-in-law; and when he moved back to his native Ireland after Patrick Brontë's death in 1861, took everything he could in the way of Charlotte's belongings (manuscripts, dresses, drawings, jewelry). He did not remarry until 1864, and even then stayed true to his dead wife's memory; when he died, aged eighty-eight, in 1906, Arthur's patient second wife, his cousin Mary Bell, placed his coffin beneath the portrait of Charlotte that hung in their drawing room, until he was carried from the house.

The Sotheby's sale the year after his death had been prompted by the fact that Mary was desperately short of money; and as the *Yorkshire Daily Observer* reported (in a cutting preserved in the museum library, and pasted inside the 1907 catalogue), "the prices ruled high," for there was much "to be coveted by worshippers at the Haworth shrine." Aside from booksellers in search of Brontë manuscripts, "there were many amateurs, British and American, and the West Riding Brontëists were well represented by Mr. Philip Unwin, flanked on either side by Mr. Clement Shorter and Mr. Wise, in whose name the bidding in the interests of the Brontë Society was made." (Shorter and T. J. Wise were also acquisitive on their own behalf, and had avidly pursued both Ellen Nussey and Arthur Bell Nicholls in their lifetimes, in search of valuable Brontë memorabilia that never came to auction; Wise was later revealed to be a forger of first editions, and maximized his profits out of the Brontës by selling off the relics and manuscripts to different private collectors.) The *Yorkshire Daily Observer* declared a small satinwood box belonging to Charlotte Brontë to be "most interesting of all"; purchased by the Brontë Society for £8 (the price noted in pencil on the catalogue that I read in the library), the box contained "a blue bead necklace, eye-glasses, and two hair bracelets with gold clasps made from the hair of her sisters Emily and Anne." Curiously, the highest price of all was paid for a relic of a relic: £32 for a fragment of Napoleon's coffin, given to Charlotte Brontë in Brussels by her teacher, Monsieur Heger (the man who she was to later fictionalize as an unlikely romantic hero).

These relics—and others, bought in an auction in 1933—are still on display in the parsonage; so I looked at them, and all the other lovingly preserved objects in the museum. There was the black horsehair sofa upon which Emily Brontë had alleg-edly died (in fact, as Juliet pointed out to me, it probably arrived after Emily's death); and the cottage piano in Patrick Brontë's study, which Emily played. Some of the mementos had been given away by Ellen Nussey and Arthur Nicholls, scattered from Haworth across the country and abroad, and then painstakingly gathered back together again; as were the fragments of Charlotte's letters that had been cut up by Patrick Brontë to satisfy persistent autograph hunters. Most of these souvenirs had colorful tales attached, such as the Italian crimping iron in the kitchen: the same one that Emily had used to cauterize a dog-bite she had received (described by Mrs. Gaskell as evidence of Emily's "nobly stern presence of mind").

I looked, too, at a copy of Branwell's portrait of his three sisters: Emily in her gigot sleeves, and the artist painted out, though his ghostly figure is reappearing in the picture, as the paint fades; and the girls' hands only barely visible, so that I could see no sign of any rings. But upstairs, in Charlotte's room, alongside the sisters' samplers, carefully sewn when they were still quite young, and Charlotte's cotton dress and boots, Juliet showed me some rings and bracelets containing interwoven locks of Brontë hair; and another ring, of gold and pearl, given to Charlotte by Arthur. (Charlotte was rather proud of her hands, reported the ever-observant Mrs. Gaskell, for they were small, slim, and beautifully shaped; which may have been why she was said to have had quite a number of rings; "one of her few personal vanities," according to a museum booklet, "as she was inordinately sensitive about her appearance which she considered to be plain to the point of ugliness.") "But nobody knows what became of her wedding ring," explained Juliet, "whether it was buried with her, or whether Arthur kept it, or possibly made certain that it would be destroyed after his death, like her wedding dress." Arthur, for all his devotion, was clearly not averse to acts of destruction, carried out—as he saw it—in order to preserve his wife's memory; and though one can understand his feelings that her wedding dress should not be feasted upon by vulture-like followers after her death, it was unfortunate that he also destroyed another of Branwell's portraits because he did not like its portrayal of his dead wife, leaving only a portion of the picture behind, of the sphinx-like Emily.

Elsewhere in the museum, we looked at the brass collars from the Brontës' dogs, engraved with their names, and a comb believed to have been dropped in the fire by Emily, when she was dying ("an unlikely story," said Juliet). And then we examined a letter to Ellen Nussey, sent from Brussels by Charlotte, in which she sketched a cartoon of herself as an ugly dwarfish figure with an oversized head, waving across the sea to a prettified Ellen, all ringlets and perfection; and Charlotte's romanticized portrait of her dead mother, drawn from an existing picture, but embellished with ribbons and lace; and Branwell's map of Angria and Glasstown, the imaginary worlds in which their early stories took place (though partly based, according to some academic researchers, on the Brontës' knowledge, gleaned through newspapers and periodicals, of English emigration to the African colonies in the 1820s).

And finally, in a glass case, were Charlotte's bonnet and wedding veil, worn for her marriage to Arthur on 29 June 1854, when the villagers who saw her coming out of Haworth church said she looked like a snowdrop. The veil, made of white netting, with a scalloped border of embroidered flowers along the edge, was given to one of the parsonage servants, Martha Brown, and passed down through her family, to her great-great-niece. "It's likely that there are many items, including jewelry, that we still don't know about," said Juliet, "that were sold privately, or given away as presents. They could have been forgotten about in a dusty attic, or preserved in a private collection. They might eventually turn up, or they might not . . ."

Afterward, back in the library, I was allowed to see one of those recent discoveries: a fragment of a letter, discovered pasted into an old autograph album, in which Charlotte Brontë described her trousseau to an unknown correspondent (possibly her friend Mrs. Gaskell, who took a keen interest in clothes). Even though I was wearing the white gloves provided by the librarian, I still took care not to touch that fragile bit of paper, but even so, it was easy to read Charlotte's neatly legible handwriting: her references to "a sort of fawn-coloured silk" and a "drab barège with a little green spot in it." When it came to describing her wedding dress, she seemed to reveal a similar hesitancy as in the earlier letter I had read, in Mrs. Gaskell's biography, about the suitability of certain colors or styles. "Nothing would satisfy some of my friends but white which I told you I would *not* wear. Accordingly they dressed me in white by way of trial—vowed away their consciences that nothing had ever suited me so well—and white I had to buy and *did* buy to my own amazement—but I took care to get it in cheap material—there were some insinuations about silk, tulle and I don't know what—but I stuck convulsively to muslin, plain book muslin with a tuck or two. Also the white veil—I took care should be a matter of 5s being simply of tulle with little tucks. If I must make a fool of myself—it shall be on an economical plan. Now I have told you all."

The partial letter had no beginning, no apparent ending, no date, no signature, and the conclusion contained within it ("Now I have told you all") was inconclusive. But what the fragment made clear, through its very obscurities, was that two hundred years after Charlotte Brontë's death, her life—for all that it had been picked over and annotated—would always remain, at its heart, unknown; for no one knew what she had written in the rest of that letter; nor what lay on the other side of the page. There was no mention of a ring in the letter, and why should there be? But there was the white muslin; and it felt like a sort of link—a magical one, I admit; as whimsical as Mr. Rochester's description of Jane Eyre as a fairy; as much of an invention as the Brontë myth—but a link, nevertheless, with my great-great-great-grandmother, Clara Lucas Balfour, who paid for her education by sewing white muslin for wedding dresses, and who had subsequently found such inspiration in Charlotte Brontë. It was the Brontës, too, who had helped give meaning to my great-aunt Madge's life in South Africa (an austere life, very different from the exciting colonial adventures of Glasstown and Angria), who in turn had inspired my mother to study literature at university; and then my mother, who passed on so much to me, who gave me *Jane Eyre* and other books to read, who made me think about wedding dresses and veils (torn or otherwise); who gave me *her* rings . . . All of a sudden, looking at that scrap of paper, I could piece these things together, books and rings and wedding dresses, the fabric of our lives, the threads of a story, and somehow, just for a few seconds, they made sense to me; briefly, they seemed to form an imaginary circle; not one that would be visible to anyone other than me.

Does that sound absurdly sentimental? Yes, it does, I know it does: and irrational and illogical as well. Which is why I didn't say anything about it to Juliet, or to the new curator, Polly Salter: but I did tell them that I had found what I had come looking for.

"Good, but you can't go back to London without seeing the storeroom," said Juliet. "That's where some of the most interesting things are . . ."

So that is where we went: me and Juliet and Polly Salter and Linda Procter-Mackley, the curatorial assistant. Polly unlocked the door, and we crowded into a small, windowless room, colder than the rest of the museum ("Temperature-controlled," murmured Juliet, "not like in my day . . .").

"We thought you should see Charlotte's going-away dress," said Polly, and she lifted a large gray cardboard box onto a table, and then put on another pair of white gloves, before unpacking the dress. "What do you think?" she said, as she carefully laid out the dress—which turned out to be a matching jacket and skirt, hand-sewn in a striped lavender silk which had faded to a dried heathery color, lined with calico.

"It's tiny," I said: and it was; made for a woman who was four foot ten, as Polly reminded me.

"You used to be able to buy a pattern of that dress," said Juliet, "here in the museum shop, so that people could sew one for themselves."

"I prefer this blue-sprigged floral dress," said Linda, uncovering another dress that was hanging on a rail at the side of the room. "It's much brighter than you'd expect, isn't it?'

"And look at the paisley one," said Juliet, "I've always thought that was pretty."

The atmosphere in the room was becoming far lighter than you might have anticipated in the inner sanctum of the museum; the initial hushed reverence in the presence of these relics giving way to something less worshipful; so that I couldn't help laughing when Juliet pointed out that the replica of Charlotte's wedding dress (copied from memory after it had been destroyed on Mr. Nicholls's instructions) looked as if it had been designed for a hobbit. Even so, it was hard not to be moved, for just as I had felt touched by Clara Lucas Balfour's diaries and notebooks—little battered things; much handled; worn soft, like papery skin—so, too, was there a kind of tenderness attached to these old dresses, so lovingly protected. Which may be why, when the curators showed me the framed and mounted locks of hair, gathered by one of the parsonage servants from the Brontë children in 1824, it seemed less ghoulish than the mourning jewelry I'd seen upstairs. Similarly, the collected scraps of material from Charlotte's dresses—framed, like the hair, as if this were a work of art; carefully labeled and attributed, and clearly matching the fabric from her trousseau—seemed benign, if doomed, evidence of a desire to preserve the living, as much as the dead.

But there was something, too, in this very material evidence of a life once lived—like the mementos elsewhere in the parsonage—that kept the house from feeling haunted (too many things, all too solid, for there to be any room for ghosts). At least, that's the way it felt to me, though Linda had stories of an earlier curator who said she had smelled the smoke from a fire in the study, despite the fact that the grate was never lit, and heard the unearthly tinkling of Emily's piano, one evening when she was alone in the museum.

"Well, I never felt anything remotely supernatural," said Juliet, briskly, "though the Brontë Society is full of people claiming to have seen visions of Emily, or saying that they're the reincarnation of Charlotte—and there was one woman who was adamant that she was the reincarnation of Charlotte's unborn baby.'

Afterward, just before I left Haworth to catch the train from Keighley back to London, I wandered round the shop attached to the Parsonage Museum. And I thought that maybe I should buy my mother a copy of one of Charlotte Brontë's rings that was on sale there: a simple plaited gold band, that reminded me of my sister's plait of hair, cut off when she was still a child, and kept by my mother in a drawer somewhere; faded now, no longer dark and glossy. "They break, those plaited rings," said Juliet, noticing my gaze.

But I'd already made my mind up not to buy the copy, to leave it be. I'd tell my mother the story so far instead, when I got home that night: another story of bits and pieces, odds and ends and off-cuts, like the framed scraps of cloth in the museum storeroom; but she'd like to hear it, anyway; she'd understand what I was talking about . . . and I was certain that it would mean more to her than the copy of another woman's ring.

16

The Black Sash

I

FOR MANY YEARS—decades, in fact, throughout my childhood, and all through adult life—I believed my maternal grand-mother to be a woman as conventional and muted as her clothes. Which is not to say that I was dismissive of her, because I loved her for her calm, considered exterior, which seemed to reflect who she was inside. My grandmother smelled of Parma violets and lavender cologne; her voice was soft as her crêpe-de-Chine tea dresses; and I never saw her anything other than fully dressed, hair brushed and the merest hint of face powder; neat as a pin, whatever the hour of day or night (not that she ever stayed up very late, as far as I could tell, except for Midnight Mass on Christmas Eve).

So it seemed almost impossible when my uncle Richard—my grandmother's first child, and my mother's older brother—told me that Pat had been a founding member of a political women's group called the Black Sash, which had campaigned against apartheid in South Africa. I was visiting him and his wife, Vicki, at the time, in July 2004, for a small family reunion at their home in Toronto (small, in that it consisted of me and my two sons, my uncle and aunt and three of their four adult children; big, in that we'd not been together since a South African Christmas when I was still a child). The boys were outside, skateboarding with my cousins Dan and David, who are in their thirties now, though fortunately able to remember their teenage pursuits; and I was sitting at the dining-room table with Richard, looking through a box full of faded sepia photographs (the remnants of a scattered family, gathered in the same place at last; though there were far more of our ancestors than us). Here was Colonel Albert Peel Garnett—my great-great-grandfather—in full Hussars regalia, and a splendid handlebar mustache—and the Colonel's son, Frederick, on his travels around Africa; and pictures of his son, my grandfather Fred, as a little boy, playing at the English seaside with his sister, Lil, in elaborate Edwardian bathing suits. And more, too, of Fred, after he had married Pat, with their three children, Richard and my mother and her twin brother; all ironed and starched and respectable, polished shoes and small smiles, their eyes narrowed against the glare of the African sun.

"It must have been such a shock for Pat and Fred," I said, "when Mum got involved in radical politics—so unexpected, I mean."

"I don't think so," said Richard. "She'd probably inherited a political streak from Pat in the first place. Haven't you heard about your grandmother's time in the Black Sash?"

I didn't know; in fact, I didn't even know what the Black Sash was, let alone why my grandmother had been a member of it, so Richard gave me the briefest of outlines, and I filled in a few more details from the Internet later that night (not that there was very much information available; for this seemed to be an organization whose history was given only the most grudging of respect). The Women's Defence of the Constitution League, which soon afterward became known as the Black Sash, was formed in Johannesburg in May 1955, at a tea party held by six middle-class white women—Jean Sinclair, Ruth Foley, Elizabeth McLaren, Tertia Pybus, Jean Bosazza and Helen Newton-Thompson—all of whom were opposed to the proposed new Senate Bill, to remove the vote from the people described in South Africa as "coloureds." At the tea party, a plan was made that each of the six women would phone another six women, friends and relatives and so on, in order to organize a series of demonstrations and silent vigils; Jean Sinclair happened to know my grandmother, who immediately agreed to join them. Richard couldn't tell me whose idea it was that they should wear black sashes, but he understood exactly what it signified: to show that they were in mourning for the constitution; which is why my grandmother sewed herself one out of cotton, worn draped over her right shoulder during protest marches. "My most vivid memory of the Black Sash is of one of their protests in Pretoria, to 'welcome' the returning Foreign Minister from an overseas visit," said Richard, who had accompanied his mother there. "Pat and all the other women formed two dignified lines on either side of the steps leading up to the government buildings. The Minister and his various aides were clearly enraged by them, and one young lout marched over to my mother and spat in her face. This caused great amusement among the ministerial party—and absolutely no intervention from any of the policemen who were hanging around to preserve the peace. I was so angry that I stepped out from behind my mother to return the insult, but she restrained me, and I always remember what she said: 'Not that way, Richard, that won't help . . .'"

As my uncle told me this story, I could picture most of what he described—him as a young man, the lines of silent women wearing their black sashes, the boy who spat in my grandmother's face, the red-faced men, laughing at her—but the piece that was missing was my grandmother. I couldn't imagine her there; not clearly, because the woman in my mind's eye was Pat as I knew her, a silvery-haired, elderly lady, a polite onlooker of the protest, not a participant. So as soon as I got back home to London from Toronto, I rang my mother, to ask her if she knew anything more than Richard did. "How come you never told me about Pat and the Black Sash before now?" I said.

"Didn't I?" she said. "Well, I'm not sure—the subject never came up, I suppose. And I was only sixteen in 1955, when my mother got involved."

"Weren't you surprised?" I said. "I find it astonishing—I thought she just went to church, and played Scrabble in the evenings, and darned Fred's socks . . ."

"You should know by now," said my mother, mildly, "that one should never judge people by appearances. But you're right, I was surprised, and proud, and it's true, she'd never seemed to me to be particularly radical before then. But my mother did have a passionate sense of injustice, and she deeply resented the Nationalist Party's attack on the old political order that she'd grown up with, even though that had been almost as repressive, in its own way. Anyway, she joined the Black Sash at the very beginning—and now that you mention it, I do remember the sash itself, watching her put it on, arranging it over her sober brown-and-blue tweed suit. That must have been the time I went with her to one of the Black Sash demonstrations—it was on the steps of the Johannesburg

City Hall, where we stood with all the other white middle-class women, in silent protest. People jeered at us, but it didn't feel dangerous to me—nobody attacked us—and I didn't think of my mother as displaying any bravery that day, but in hindsight, she was quite courageous, and I'm grateful for it as one of the radicalizing events in my life. I remember talking to my mother on the way home—about the tactics of peaceful protest, and Gandhi, who had lived in South Africa as a young lawyer—in fact, we knew exactly where he'd lived, because some friends of the family had moved into the same house."

My mother paused, but only very briefly—which is not like her; I usually have to prompt her to talk, instead of listening to others; but this time, she still had more to tell me. "Two or three years later, after that day at the City Hall, I had become more involved in campaigning against the Nationalist Government bill enforcing segregation in the universities. I was at university myself by then, and the Black Sash seemed terribly tame and bourgeois to me—and of course, my parents were very worried by what I was getting up to, by my involvement with what they thought of as a dangerous and reckless opposition, with people who were prepared to go to prison for their beliefs. Yes, my mum was still involved with the Black Sash, but she saw that as being completely different from the revolutionaries I was meeting at university." My mother laughed, and said, "I wasn't particularly brave, and I was only on the fringes of the struggle against apartheid, but I was arrested at a party one night, along with everyone else. Fortunately, the case was thrown out of court, and I escaped from South Africa at the very end of 1959, before getting into any more trouble, took the Union Castle boat from Cape Town to Southampton, and arrived in London with £50 in my pocket—which wasn't even enough for a return fare home."

"And what about Pat and the Black Sash?" I asked.

"She gave it up when she moved to Cape Town, soon after I'd left the country," said my mother.

"Because it had become too political by then?" I asked.

"No, for the same reason that she abandoned most of her other activities," said my mother. "She was terribly humiliated by the fact that my twin brother had been arrested on fraud charges, and she wanted anonymity—she couldn't face any of the people she'd known."

I was almost as surprised by my mother's words as I had been by Richard's revelation about the Black Sash: for it is very rare for my mother to mention her twin; a man I've met less than a handful of times, who played no part in the family stories I heard when I was growing up. In fact, it was a long time before I even realized she had a twin; though on odd occasions I was aware of something unspoken—a hesitation, an uncomfortable silence. And when, at ten or eleven, I became aware of her missing twin, his absence did not take a neutral form; it was an absence that had a presence to it, like a quicksand, into which I feared that my mother might disappear; all the more dangerous because it remained unseen.

Her silence on the subject of her twin brother was only partly similar to my grandparents' manner of dealing with him; when he was absent from their lives, which he often was, they made no reference to the reason why he had gone, or where he might be; when he returned, they adored him, without question. So although I had eventually guessed, from my mother's guarded and cryptic remarks, that her twin might have been in prison at some point in his life, it was only now, in this conversation, that my suspicion was confirmed. But oddly, the fact that my unknown uncle had been a criminal seemed unrelated to me—as distant, almost, as my grandmother's great-uncle Jabez. What seemed closer—more urgent—was why my grandmother had given up the Black Sash, and taken on another form of silent mourning, of an entirely solitary kind; why her sense of shame, of innocence undone, had made her give up her ideals; as if she was the one who had been exposed as fraudulent.

"My twin brother had gone to prison when I was at university," my mother continued, "but I didn't know that then—and Pat and Fred either didn't know, or didn't want to know, and they never said a word about it to me. But afterward, when he got out, there were other incidents, other court cases—and the disgrace that my mother felt was so acute that she wanted to get away from everyone who knew her in Johannesburg, which is why they moved to Cape Town."

"Did you ever visit him in prison?" I asked, not wanting my mother to stop talking.

"Once," she said, "not long after you'd left home, to go to university. He was in for fraud . . . It was so painful to see him there, but he said, 'Oh, don't worry about me—I'm an old con.' And of course, he had conned everyone—my parents, my aunts—he stole from them all."

"Why was he like that?" I said; because it seemed impossible that twins should be so different (although my mother has been rebellious, she is the most honorable and upright of women; indeed, her rebellion has its bedrock in belief).

"I'm not sure," she replied. "I think he spent time in several psychiatric hospitals—my father once admitted to that—and he was diagnosed with a personality disorder. But I always felt

225

as if it was my fault: he was born with a broken leg, you see, and the story I was told from the start was that I'd broken his leg, which of course made me feel guilty about him, as if I were the wicked twin. Later, much later, I was trying to talk about him to my mother—trying to make her acknowledge that he was stealing from them—and she said, 'If you think bad things about him, you'll make them come true.' And you know, they really loved him—more than Richard or me, because they felt we'd both abandoned them when we left South Africa—but he was the prodigal son, and when he came back, he always told the most fabulous stories, and they always believed him—it was an article of faith for my parents, that if they believed him, all would be well."

The last time she'd seen him, she said, was when we had gone to South Africa for my grandfather's ninetieth birthday party, in 1994. She had flown there from America with her second husband, who was still alive at the time, though very ill with AIDS, and Ruth and I had traveled together from London, with my sons; and my mother's twin brother had been there, charming and funny and bright; altogether so immensely likable that it seems surprising he was not more successful in his career as a con man; that he had ever been caught, and convicted, and jailed. But I couldn't see my mother's face reflected in his, nor the other way round; you could not say that he was her shadow side; the division was too complete for that, "I've only spoken to him once since then," said my mother, "when he rang me on our sixtieth birthday. I didn't know what to say. Ruth had died, our parents were dead—and I felt like I didn't know him, my own twin brother—I just know that he's lived a shadowy life since early adulthood. It's a great hole in my life—a blank, like a history book full of empty pages. He might be a completely reformed character, or he might be dead by now, but I wouldn't know. He might need help, he might be in desperate need—but how could I give it to him?"

II

When I decided to go back to South Africa, to Cape Town, more than ten years after my last trip there, it wasn't because I thought I could find my mother's twin brother for her. I didn't think that was my job; and anyway, it didn't seem to me that she felt it necessary to look for him, nor that he wanted to be found. But I did want to go back to the place my parents had come from; and I wanted my husband and children to see Cape Town, where I had gone on childhood holidays for years, visiting Pat and Fred annually; to go up Table Mountain again, as I had done with my grandparents, and gaze beyond that ridge, where more ranges of mountains stretch away into the ash-blue distance; and to feel the wind that whips up the cold Atlantic waves, and look up into the unfamiliar night sky of the southern hemisphere, where the stars make different signs.

And I wanted, also, to see if there were some traces remaining of my grandmothers: Pat, who had fled here from Johannesburg; and Minnie, who had come to Cape Town as a child, arriving on the *Union Castle* steamship from England, having first made the long journey to London from Lithuania. I'd had a sense of unease about the trip—an anxiety that I couldn't put a name to; not just the old remembered guilt about being white in South Africa—but I was excited, too; and when we arrived after an overnight flight, landing in the African morning, I felt as if I had come to the right place; that I was not mistaken in making this return.

The city had changed out of all recognition, of course; with freeways and flyovers and multimillion-pound marina penthouses, though the squatter camps on the road coming in from the airport looked just the same; the dark poverty spilling out of corrugated-iron shacks. And there were the same startling contrasts I remembered from before, between the abundant beauty of the landscape and the squalor of the city's hidden places; where the difference between being black and being white appeared as inescapable as it ever was, even though I was an outsider, and had no right to say so, even though I knew this was the New South Africa, the rainbow nation, where people talked about looking to the future, not the past.

But the past came rushing up toward me—not in the monochrome of photographs from a family album; but here and now, urgent and impossible; chaotic and elusive and reflected in the sunlight; refracted in the curve of the sky and the sea. And the mountains were still there—the Twelve Apostles beyond Table Mountain, that Pat had counted out for me—and the hotel we were staying in was on a quay overlooking Table Bay, close to where the ships had docked, bringing my grandparents here, taking my mother away. And it seemed extraordinary to be in this city—that felt both foreign and familiar—on the other side of the world from my home, thousands of miles and over a hundred years apart from my Jewish grandparents' homeland, and from the England that my maternal grandparents held so dear: yet this was the only place we had in common; this was our common ground.

I'd hoped that in coming here, I might also find a record of

Minnie's journey to Cape Town, and my grandfather's, in the Jewish Museum of South Africa, which has a computer database containing the names of 56,000 emigrants who passed through the Poor Jews' Temporary Shelter in the East End of London, and another thousand Jewish names from the shipping manifests. As it turned out, I could find neither of them in the records; but there was a mass of interesting material in the rest of the museum, which is housed in the first synagogue to be built in South Africa, consecrated in 1863. I looked at prayer shawls and swaddling cloths; old suitcases and traveling trunks; a peddler's cart full of buttons, beads, pins, brooches and gloves (because many of the first Jewish settlers in South Africa had started out making a living as "smous," the Afrikaans word for itinerant peddlers, traveling between the small towns, or "drops," until they could save enough capital to set up a permanent shop, like my father's paternal grandfather, Moses, who eventually established a men's tailoring store). And I read about Max Rose, a Lithuanian Jewish immigrant dubbed the ostrich-feather king of South Africa, whose enormous success drew many other Lithuanians to follow him to Oudtshoorn, an ostrichfarming boomtown in the Karoo desert of Western Cape which became the center of the world feather industry, complete with splendid Gothic mansions known as feather palaces, built by millionaires who had made their fortune out of boas and fans and plumed hats; until the crash in 1914, when feathers went out of fashion, and Max Rose lost his fortune, like the other ostrich barons, and "the Jerusalem of Africa" went back to being plain Oudtshoorn again.

Finally, in another gallery, darker and more melancholy than the others, I saw the reconstructed "shtet," based on the

Lithuanian villages that many of the Jewish arrivals in Cape Town had left behind; with exhibits of their traditional craftsmanship, the handwork of the tailors, weavers and shoemakers who had fled the Russian pogroms of 1881. And I wondered, then, if that might be why needles and thread and feathers and shoes had always seemed so important to me; that even though I had no real access to my father's Jewish past, its apparently inconsequential bits and pieces and fripperies had somehow, mysteriously, become dear to my heart. ("Why can't you tell me more about Minnie and Rosa?" I'd said to him, before going to South Africa. "How can so much of their stories have been lost?" "I've tried to explain to you before," he said, patiently. "They didn't talk about the past— the past was hidden, because they felt guilty—because of all those relatives who were left behind in Europe, who died in the pogroms and the Holocaust.")

After I left the Jewish Museum, I had another appointment, with Jenny de Tolly, one of the current trustees of the Black Sash (which has survived as an advice organization, and has its headquarters in Cape Town). It might sound like a wild goose chase—from ostrich feathers to a black sash; from one grandmother to another—but it made enough sense to me. (These were my grandmothers, after all; I was their common ground, as well as the city being ours; they had a meeting place within me.) I'd arranged to see Jenny at her home in the suburbs—not far from where my mothers' parents had lived when I was a child; though now the houses on these quiet streets were hidden behind high walls, and notices warning of twenty-four-hour armed security. Jenny's house was one of only two on her road not to have a fence around it, or iron gates, and she welcomed me with a warmth that I had not expected, as a stranger; showing me her old black sash, sewn of soft cotton, and the filmed interviews she'd had the foresight to do a dozen or so years ago, of the older, early members of the organization, my grandmother's peers, nearly all of whom were now dead. We sat, side by side, on the sofa in her front room, and watched the film, which included an interview with Jean Sinclair, who had recruited my grandmother to the Black Sash, and who talked about how fast the word had spread, with a petition of 100,000 signatures gathered in ten days. There were other women, too, who looked like my grandmother had when I first knew her—all very properly turned out and respectably dressed—remembering what they called "the hauntings," when they shadowed government ministers in their black sashes. "We went in our best silk dresses and stockings," said one of them, "and then got our sashes out of our handbags, before anyone could stop us." Another of them, a Cape Town florist named Joan Pare, described the code she had worked out with a Johannesburg florist who also supported the Black Sash, to get the organizational messages and information relayed across the country, when their telephones were being tapped: "all the ministers were given different code names, after flowers, so we would send telegrams to each other saying, 'Have sent pink carnation on train, meet at station at 2pm,' and that meant we would know to get everyone together to haunt the relevant minister at the appointed time."

And they talked about how they'd used flowers, also, after being banned from wearing their black sashes in demonstrations outside the Parliament buildings in Cape Town: pinning black fabric roses to their bosoms instead; and inside Parliament, in the public gallery, they wore long black gloves, and stitched sashes across their blouses, which could not be removed. None of them made reference to the suffragettes, though as I watched the film, it was hard not to compare the two movements, at least in their symbolic use of clothes; the suffragettes in their white and green and purple outfits, with hats and banners to match (purple to represent their dignity, white for purity, green for hope). But the Black Sash was more peaceful, and also less successful than the suffragettes. Their protests did not prevent the Senate Act from being passed, nor from the inexorable spread of more apartheid laws, yet many remained committed to the campaign, carrying placards declaring: "The Case Is Lost But Not The Cause" and "Legal Now But Immoral Forever."

"We couldn't shut up shop," said Jean Sinclair (a dead woman remembering the past, speaking to me in Jenny de Tolly's front room), "so we decided to keep going, and to protest against all the unjust laws. And when that happened, I lost most of my friends . . ."

"Husbands felt very neglected," added Joan Pare, surrounded by the flowers of her florist shop (and yes, said Jenny, Joan had died, too). "My husband came down to breakfast one morning wearing my black sash, staging a protest because I hadn't sewn any buttons onto his shirts . . ."

"That's when the political became personal," remarked Jenny. "And can you imagine the conversations at home, when these very respectable ladies, married to very respected businessmen, who had got themselves invited to the opening of Cape Town airport, pulled their black sashes out of their handbags, when the government minister stepped off the first plane?"

III

The Black Sash went out of fashion, superseded by more radical organizations like the ANC, yet has not been entirely forgotten—when I visited Jenny, she was helping to plan its fiftieth-anniversary celebrations for May 2005. But my grandmothers' names were nowhere to be found in Cape Town; their joys and their sorrows left no material mark; they came and they went, unremembered on war memorials or in museums, not hailed as heroines, their struggles too small to be listed for posterity, their personal lives insufficiently political in a city where apartheid can never be forgotten, where Robben Island is always in view if you look out to Table Bay, an inescapable reminder of Nelson Mandela's long imprisonment there.

No one knows what became of Pat's hand-sewn black sash; not my mother, nor her cousin Molly, Hope's daughter, who still lives in Cape Town. ("So much disappeared," Molly told me, when we met for breakfast one morning, "all Pat's jewelry after she died, those few bits that were left, because most of it had already gone, and Pat and Fred's wedding photographs, which is a shame, because I was a flower-girl when they got married, and I'd have loved for you to see those pictures.")

At least I have the garnet brooch that my mother bought for Pat when I was born, and which my grandmother then gave to me; but I have nothing solid of Minnie's to remember her by; no ring, no jewels, not even a thimble, just the photographs at home on my mantelpiece, the one of her on her wedding day; the other, an elderly lady in a thick coat and hat and scarf and gloves, bundled up against the unfamiliar cold of an English springtime, an umbrella in one hand, my hand in the other. I am three years old, or thereabouts; my sister has just been born, and Minnie has come to visit us. There is a door behind us, and a wall covered in clematis or magnolia flowers. I am wearing a shapeless hat and a dark coat so that I look like a small version of her; in this indistinct photograph (black and white and gray) it is our clothes that mark us as related, not the details of our faces. It is the clothes that are the only clue to what has passed between us.

But I have left home, left the photographs behind, and come to Cape Town, where my grandmothers once were; where they *lived*; I have come here, because of them. Yet the past will not uncover itself in the way I had imagined; though perhaps imagination is as important here; and the knowledge that old shames and secrets are not what I will take home with me; that, and the belief that my grandmothers were not nobodies; they lived and breathed and laughed and cried, like their children, and their children's children; they are the underside of the tapestry of my life (pick it up, turn it over, look more closely, and they are there).

And when I find myself, toward the end of our visit to South Africa, by my younger son's bed in a hospital room— nothing serious, it turns out, but one of the usual run of accidents and mishaps that mark a family's narrative—I think of my grandmothers, and my mother, and all the times they sat through a long night like this one, waiting for another dark- ness to turn to dawn. I stroke my fingers over my son's cheek, just to check that he is breathing; yes, my child is sleeping, he is safe, even though sometimes it seems as if everything that is precious hangs on a thread. A nurse comes in at the start of each hour, to check his temperature and blood pressure; time passes, time stands still again. I am wearing the same clothes from last night, when we rushed him to the hospital—a black Ghost top and trousers, my sister's black Gap jacket; all in black, in this pale hospital room, where my son lies covered in a white sheet, where I watch him breathing, evenly; red hair just visible, unfaded against his golden-brown skin. In my ears are the moonstone studs that my husband bought me, four days ago, as a present on Valentine's Day; and on my fingers are my mother's rings that her father gave to her; and my wedding ring, and a diamond engagement ring, a present from my husband after we were married, after my first engagement ring lost its pearl. (Are pearls unlucky, I think to myself, nearly dreaming, after a night sitting awake in this hospital chair . . .)

Six-fifteen in the morning, and the sun is rising in Cape Town, dawn is breaking over Signal Hill. The sky is high and blue, the light is bright and clear, and at last, I almost understand, at long last, why my mother chose a black wedding dress, less than a year after she had left South Africa, after she had left her mother in mourning, after she had left her twin brother behind; a black dress, to wear beneath a leaden foreign sky, where rain turned into fog, and the sun was a low and sullen thing.

There are no curtains on the wide hospital window, and the birds are flying past; we're on the tenth floor, and I can see them swooping and wheeling and diving, gulls and swallows and swifts and pigeons, up and away, wings spread wide and perfectly balanced, fast and brave and beautiful. ("Free as the air," my mother used to say, reminding my sister and I when we were little girls to look up from the ground, "the birds are free as the air . . .")

I couldn't tell where we were in the hospital last night, couldn't get my bearings in this city, but now I can see the brightly colored houses outside in Bo-Kaap, unmistakable landmarks on the sides of Signal Hill; the Cape Malay houses, painted burnt orange and lime green and turquoise and lilac; rose pink and lemon yellow and ochre and celadon. I list the rainbow of colors to myself, and I remember what my grandmother told me as a child: that the Muslim slaves painted these houses when they gained their freedom; they celebrated in this way, they chose their own colors, their independence was splashed out for all to see. (I don't know if Pat's version of history is accurate; but it seems like an interesting story to tell, in a country that was governed and carved up according to the surface of things; where color was seen as more than skin deep.)

It's all a patchwork, I think, eyes closing against the light; all of this, it could be torn into pieces so easily; slit the threads, and everything falls apart (the fragile peace of the rainbow nation; the happiness of a single family). But we are still here; the stitches still hold; that which is precious is not yet broken. My child is sleeping, and I am with him; my son is safe, and out of the window I can see this place that others have called the Mother City.

And they're all here, just for one moment, in this moment, clothed in sunlight, all of them. My grandmothers and my mother and my sister, here with me now in the Cape Town dawn.

Acknowledgments

This is a book written with the help of many others: first and foremost, my mother, Hilary Britten, and my father, Michael Picardie. Other relatives were also generous with their time and memories: my uncle and aunt Richard and Vicki Garnett; my mother's cousin Molly Green; Jan de Crespigny; and Janet Cunliffe-Jones, whose research into my great-great-great-grandmother Clara Lucas Balfour deserves a book of its own.

Many thanks, also, to friends and colleagues at *Vogue*: to Alexandra Shulman, who has been the most steadfast of editors; Fran Bentley, Lucinda Chambers, Jo Craven, Anna Cryer, Susie Forbes, Chloe Fox, Fiona Golfar, Francesca Martin, Harriet Quick, Emily Sheffield, Anna-Marie Solowij and Kim Stringer. They have been unfailingly generous in offering advice, information and access to the fashion industry; as have Jo Allison, Anita Borzyszkowska, Tracey Boyd, Julieanne Dorff, Lulu Guinness, Sydney Ingle-Finch, Betty Jackson, Bernadette Rendall and Tanya Sarne.

I am similarly grateful to Michele Lavery, the editor of the Saturday *Telegraph* magazine, who commissioned me to write about Karl Lagerfeld and Donatella Versace (interviews I have subsequently drawn on here); Kathryn Holliday, deputy editor of the Saturday *Telegraph* magazine; and other *Telegraph* editors, past and present, who have given me the space to think about fashion, including Georgina Cover, Rachel Forder, Sarah Sands, Emma Soames, Lucy Tuck, Rebecca Tyrrel and Cathy Wilson.

Thanks, too, for encouragement, patience, facts, suggestions and insight: Juliet Barker, Sophie Dahl, Rupert Everett, Bella Freud, Amanda Harlech, Nick Hornby, Nigella Lawson, Kay Marles, Erin O'Connor, Maggie O'Farrell, Adam Phillips and Polly Samson.

I would like to thank the staff of the Brontë Parsonage Museum for their invaluable help and expertise, and for access to the museum archives; Rebecca Fraser, President of the Brontë Society; and Kathryn Spink, who was kind enough to send me a copy of her book, *Black Sash: The Beginning of a Bridge in South Africa*.

Many, many thanks, as ever, to my agent, Ed Victor, my editor, Imogen Taylor, and to Nicholas Blake, Camilla Elworthy, Trisha Jackson, Andrew Kidd and Stephanie Sweeney at Picador.

Neill, Jamie, and Tom: best companions to the other side of the wardrobe and beyond; and Ruth, my sister, always . . .

Permissions

A NOTE ON THE AUTHOR

Justine Picardie is a journalist, novelist and editor. She is the author of *If the Spirit Moves You: Life and Love After Death* and the novel *Wish I May*, and the cowriter or editor of several other books. She was formerly the features editor of British *Vogue* and editor of the *Observer* magazine. She lives in London with her husband and two sons.

A NOTE ON THE TYPE

The text of this book is set in Linotype Sabon, named after the type founder, Jacques Sabon. It was designed by Jan Tschichold and jointly developed by Linotype, Monotype and Stempel, in response to a need for a typeface to be available in identical form for mechanical hot metal composition and hand composition using foundry type.

Tschichold based his design for Sabon roman on a font engraved by Garamond, and Sabon italic on a font by Granjon. It was first used in 1966 and has proved an enduring modern classic.